T0323598

Cambridge Elements ☰

Elements in Philosophy of Law
edited by
George Pavlakos
University of Glasgow
Gerald J. Postema
University of North Carolina at Chapel Hill
Kenneth M. Ehrenberg
University of Surrey

THE NORMATIVITY
OF LAW

Michael Giudice
York University

CAMBRIDGE
UNIVERSITY PRESS

Contents

Introduction

It might be tempting to begin a work on the normativity of law by stating in a succinct and pithy way *the* precise problem to which an account of the normativity of law is meant as an answer, to draw out *the* common conception of the problem of the normativity of law across different eras and perspectives. This will not be my approach, neither as a starting point nor a destination. The problem of the normativity of law is many, not one, and this is as it should be. Law – including its normativity – is interesting for several reasons and from diverse angles. A core aim of this Element is therefore quite modest: to map some of the numerous ways in which the problem of the normativity of law has been conceived and answered. Another aim will be to show some of the pitfalls of failing to observe the differences.

The expression "normativity of law" has no home in ordinary language; it is entirely a product of legal theory, and most likely legal philosophy in particular. And within legal philosophy, it has been understood in various ways, giving rise to various kinds of investigations with various goals. It would therefore be quite remarkable if, despite all appearances, legal philosophers working on the normativity of law were somehow all best understood as engaged in identical pursuits. Legal philosophers are, after all, a disagreeable bunch. They love to find fault, not just in the details but also with the entire character and objectives of each other's views. A brief survey should help to illustrate.

Early statements of the problem of the normativity of law took their cue from the normative language used in law, such as rights, obligations, duties, and responsibilities. Joseph Raz, for example, writes, "The problem of the normativity of law is the problem of explaining the use of normative language in describing the law or legal situations" (Raz, 1999, 170). Similarly, H. L. A. Hart notes, "I share with [Kelsen] the conviction that a central task of legal philosophy is to explain the normative force of propositions of law which figure both in academic legal writing and in the discourse of judges and lawyers" (Hart, 1983, 18). Hart was of course writing during a time when ordinary language philosophy was in its heyday, and though Raz framed his early work in the same way, it was not long until his approach became primarily one of practical philosophy, a special branch of philosophy concerned with the nature and operation of reasons for action. The prominence of practical philosophy as a way of doing legal philosophy itself gave rise to new statements and framings of the problem of the normativity of law. We find, for example, Gerald Postema elaborating on what he takes to be the problem that Hart (and Raz) have identified:

> A central task of philosophical jurisprudence is to explain and reconcile two
> (sometimes apparently conflicting) sets of widely shared beliefs about our

legal practices. On the one hand, we recognize that the notion of law is essentially practical. "Law" lives in the familiar environment of "rights," "obligations," "reasonableness," and their cognates, all of which derive their distinctive character from the roles they play in the practical deliberation and guidance of rational agents ... On the other hand, we believe that law is essentially a social phenomenon – a complex of social institutions which can be studied by external observers and participants viewing their practices as external observers ... The problem of accounting for the normativity of law is the task of explaining, illuminating, and where necessary reconciling these beliefs. (Postema, 1987, 81)

In Scott Shapiro's work, an additional dimension is introduced to the problem of the normativity of law. In commenting on Hart's positivist theory, Shapiro articulates the problem in this way, which puts a key inference (or derivation) at the center: "How can normative judgments about legal rights and obligations be derived from purely descriptive judgments about social practices?" (Shapiro, 2011, 97). I shall suggest later that supposing there is an inference here that needs to be made and defended is a mistake; it not only distorts Hart's view but marks a significant misdirection of efforts. But for now it is worth continuing the brief survey.

Others, such as Fred Schauer, see much less of a problem for legal theory:

Legal philosophers since Hart have tended to accept this account of how law can create obligations [that people take an internal point of view toward their legal rules], but they often make it more mysterious than necessary, typically by describing the issue in terms of a genuine puzzle about the source of law's "normativity." But the issue is not nearly as puzzling as these theorists would have us believe. Whenever we are inside a rule system, we have obligations created by that system. (Schauer, 2015, 33–34)

Schauer goes on to explain that morality, religion, chess, etiquette, and fashion, just like law, are systems of norms that, once accepted or internalized, give rise to system-relative obligations: "[i]f one accepts – internalizes, or takes as a guide to action – the system, then that system can create obligations for those who accept it" (Schauer, 2015, 34).

Though I sympathize with Schauer's view, it might be too swift to adopt such a relativistic understanding of normativity – that normativity is always categorized into some single domain and conditioned on acceptance or internalization. Questions remain. Is there something distinctive about how different types of norms create obligations? For example, obligations of fashion seem wholly conditional on acceptance, but is the same true of moral obligations? Is the normativity of obligations in one domain to be explained (even in part) by drawing on resources from other domains of normativity?

These are only a few statements, all drawn from just one subfield of analytical legal philosophy: they are all attempts to make sense of the problem of the normativity of law as Hart conceived it. Hart is of course not the whole of legal philosophy, so other views will be surveyed. As we will see, as soon as we broaden our scope, the range of views can quickly become truly dizzying. The first aim of this Element is therefore to survey, though not exhaustively, the diversity of conceptions of the problem of the normativity of law. A second aim will be to highlight some of the dangers (wasted energies and misadventures) of failing to observe such diversity.

There are not only different answers to the problem of the normativity of law, but different conceptions of what the problem is. I believe they fall into three general categories, which I shall treat as individually defensible and necessary[1] for investigations into understanding the normativity of law. My approach could therefore be described as, at the risk of using an overused term, *pluralistic*. The three categories are (i) *conceptual or analytical*, which investigates, using descriptive–explanatory methods, the foundations of legal normativity and the distinct kind(s) of normative claims law purports to make; (ii) *evaluative*, which investigates, using forms of critical assessment, the reasons officials have to create, apply, and enforce some laws as opposed to others, and the reasons nonofficials have to comply with law or not (while there may be many such reasons, I shall focus on moral and prudential reasons); and (iii) *empirical*, which investigates, using tools from the natural and social sciences, the empirical (which includes causal and cultural) contexts of law's normative claims and effects. There are, of course, relations between these categories, but such relations are compatible with their distinctness. Most importantly, collapsing one approach into another is to be avoided; they are each irreducibly basic.

It is not my view, however, that there is no common topic across diverse views. While not all theorists agree on what the problem of the normativity of law is, those to be surveyed can all be understood in one way or another as concerned with explaining the relation between law and reason. What I want to insist on, however, is that a common topic does not amount to identity of particular questions, identity of conceptions of the problem, or identity of methodological approaches. Not all theorists are asking and answering the same question or problem, or using the same methods. The different categories of investigation – conceptual, evaluative, and empirical – each offer something of distinct importance and value, which together combine for a balanced and broad understanding of law's normativity. This ought to be a matter of course,

---

[1] I deliberately refrain from saying "jointly sufficient," for there may be other general ways of exploring the normativity of law. While I shall try to be as capacious as possible in subsequent sections, I make no claim to being comprehensive.

but unfortunately it requires defense. This will be another aim I set out to accomplish: that questions about the normativity of law are not limited to conceptual or philosophical questions, but cover a much wider range of disciplines and types of investigation. Simply put, to suppose that the problem of the normativity of law is solely a philosophical problem is a mistake.

This Element is divided into three parts. In Part I (Sections 1–4), I provide a survey of various conceptions of the problem of the normativity of law across a highly selective sampling from within the history of Western legal theory (though not so selective that the sampling cannot serve its purpose in identifying some core ideas, themes, and differences). This first part, perhaps unsurprisingly, will be devoted to examination of natural law theory and legal positivism. What might be surprising, however, is that I shall not follow the conventional approach of identifying and dwelling on the disagreements between natural law theorists and legal positivists. Instead, I shall emphasize the similarities, as there is much to learn by appreciating these. I therefore focus on the long-standing debate between natural law theory and legal positivism, not out of blind adherence to this common way of framing issues in the philosophy of law, but rather to show that the kind of reasonable diversity in legal philosophy I seek to highlight can be found even here, despite prevailing urges to see nothing but opposition.

Section 1 presents some key aspects of the natural law theories of Aristotle, St. Thomas Aquinas, and John Finnis. Each notes that human, positive law has a special force, but in a way that is tied to moral standards external and prior to its existence. On their accounts, explanation of law's moral normativity, or the moral dimension to law's normativity, is essential to explanation of the normativity of law, given the nature of law.

Section 2 highlights key claims in the views of early positivists such as Thomas Hobbes, Jeremy Bentham, and John Austin, who, in slightly different ways, focused attention on the distinctive place of human law in securing obedience through the use of threats of sanction. Their views will simply be introduced in this section. In Section 7, I will return to the relation between law and coercion, and explain why coercion – including some dominant views to the contrary – also forms an essential part of explaining the normativity of law.

In Section 3, I present some elements of the views of Hans Kelsen and H. L. A. Hart. Both Kelsen and Hart attempted to isolate, in more general terms than their predecessors, the precise way in which law stands as a special category of normative thought or special kind of reason for action. Both were also engaged in investigations into the foundations of legal order, which for Kelsen had to be presumed, and for Hart had to be socially created. They agreed that the normativity of law required explanation of the place of individual legal norms in legal systems (to explain the distinct kind of "oughtness" of legal norms), but they disagreed on how this explanation went: Kelsen thought sociology and psychology could play no role in explaining the normative character of law, while for Hart these social sciences, or at least the kinds of facts upon which they were built, were essential to understanding the existence, character, and normativity of law.

In Section 4, I outline some of the elements of Joseph Raz's view of law as a special kind of practical reason – namely, a kind of second-order reason that is meant, and claims, to play a distinctive role in the practical reasoning of subjects. I believe Raz's emphasis on the claim to legitimate authority, together with emphasis on the conditions of truth of that claim, present a valuable example of the kind of pluralism about the normativity of law that we would do well to observe.

Part II (Sections 5–7) turns to critical examination of what I take to be some misguided steps in work on the normativity of law. In Section 5, I examine so-called third theories or antipositivist theories of law – those of Ronald Dworkin and Lon Fuller – which try to generate law's normativity by examining its internal morality (whether substantive or procedural). While there is great value in their theories, their conception of the normativity of law, cast as the task of deriving moral value from within law itself, misses the mark, and needlessly so. Theirs is a mistake of collapsing the problem of the normativity of law into just one problem, and of expecting too much from a single kind of approach.

In Section 6, I turn to recent positivist accounts of law, focusing here on those that try to generate "robust," "real," or "genuine" normative reasons from social facts alone. These accounts turn to developments in philosophy more broadly, such as work on "shared cooperative activities" or "artifacts," to explain law's normativity in a way free from moral assessment. I shall argue that the problem with these theories is, remarkably, of the same kind as the problem with Dworkin's and Fuller's view: they attempt to generate too much normativity from within the practice of law itself. They would do better, I argue, to connect questions of law's claim to moral normativity with investigations that draw directly from wider and more external sources of reasons.

In Section 7, I consider some recent debates about the relation between law and coercion, here suggesting that while the conceptual question about whether law and coercion are necessarily connected is important, its central role in legal theory has had the unfortunate effect of excluding empirical questions about law's coercive force as irrelevant to investigations about the normativity of law. This is a significant misstep in need of correction.

Part III (Sections 8 and 9) looks back and forward. In Section 8, I collect the observations and lessons drawn from Sections 1 to 7 and sketch some ways of thinking pluralistically about the normativity of law. Section 9 then ventures ahead to where I think new and important directions lie.

Two preliminary notes should be added about the approach taken in this Element. First, my focus in Parts I and II is what could be called major-figure-centric. This is not meant to be disrespectful of the work of contemporary theorists who offer important and nuanced elaborations of the views of Hart, Dworkin, and Raz, among others, but only to suggest that there are some key lessons still to be learned by returning to these key figures. Second, for the most part, I will not go deeply into particular contemporary disputes as these have grown and developed. One reason is space, as this is only a short work, but the other is skepticism that depth is always a sound metatheoretical principle, especially when pursued with too much enthusiasm or for its own sake. Sometimes, a really deep account just takes us down a really deep hole, with no additional insight. More importantly, really deep accounts often ignore key first steps or observations that can prove much more valuable.

PART I

1 The Moral Normativity of Law: Aristotle, Aquinas, Finnis

This section will highlight three familiar natural law theorists – Aristotle, St. Thomas Aquinas, and John Finnis – whose sustained views have come to shape mainstream natural law theory in the Western and European tradition in many ways. The goal will not be to defend any of their particular views, but to introduce (and, I will confess, endorse) the general idea that a necessary part of understanding the normativity of human law must lie outside of human law itself. The key claim for each of Aristotle, Aquinas, and Finnis is that moral evaluation is a necessary dimension to investigation of the normativity of law – what we might call law's moral normativity. Or, in other words, it is an essential part of understanding the normativity of law that we understand under what conditions there are moral reasons to create, apply, enforce, and obey law. As such, the theories of Aristotle, Aquinas, and Finnis can all be understood as *evaluative* theories, and specifically *morally evaluative* theories, as outlined in the Introduction.

1.1 Aristotle

Though the expression "normativity of law" is relatively recent, as a general topic in the philosophy of law it is very old and dates back at least to the ancient Greeks. Aristotle, for example, draws a distinction between two types of justice or rules, precisely along the lines of the different sources of their force:

Of political justice part is natural, part legal – natural, that which everywhere has the same force and does not exist by people's thinking this or that; legal, that which is originally indifferent, but when it has been laid down is not indifferent, e.g. that a prisoner's ransom shall be a mina, or that a goat and not two sheep shall be sacrificed . . . (Aristotle, 2009, 92)

Aristotle was of course among the first natural law theorists and set out to explain the binding force of human-made law precisely in terms of how well it provided the conditions for humans to attain their natural perfection: a life of virtue and flourishing. Aristotle believed humans were indeed special, but not so special that our laws stood somehow outside of the natural order of the world, which was to be understood with a teleological metaphysics through and through. In nature Aristotle observed balance, harmony, and the absence of excess as conducive to flourishing, and reasoned that human laws ought also to strive at balance, harmony, and the means to create and maintain the conditions for human flourishing. The problem of the normativity of law was therefore conceived very early as recognition of external or prior constraints on fallible human laws, which gave human laws their reason and purpose. This is the hallmark of natural law theory. While conceptions of natural law have changed and varied, they all share this basic structure and idea: that there are objective, universal standards and values, and these constrain and act as the binding force of any justified laws humans might make for themselves.

1.2 St. Thomas Aquinas

The natural law theory of Aquinas takes a similar structure to Aristotle's, but with an important difference. Aquinas also believed that there are natural, objective moral standards that all human laws must match to be morally binding and obligatory, but for Aquinas these standards originate from a theistic, and in particular Christian, worldview: for human laws to be binding and have normative force, they must conform to the natural law, understood as a system of principles of reason divinely designed for humans and discoverable through rational reflection.

But more important than this difference, Aquinas drew a similar distinction to Aristotle's between natural justice and legal (or conventional) justice. In Aquinas's work, this is the difference between the natural law and human laws. The two ways in which human laws are to be derived from the natural law are essential to understanding Aquinas's view about the normativity of law. The first is by way of deduction, or simple syllogism, where a major premise and a minor premise combine to produce one, and only one, conclusion. Aquinas offers a familiar example of this type of derivation: the conclusion that "one must not kill," a common human law, is derived deductively from the natural law principle that "one should do harm to no man" (major premise) and the fact or observation that "killing is an instance of harm" (minor premise) (Aquinas, 2017, 39). In this example, the normative force or bindingness of the human law derives entirely from its source in the natural law. The second form of derivation, however, centers the force or bindingness of human laws on human laws themselves. In what Aquinas refers to as "*determinatio*," the exercise of choice is required, and introduces some arbitrariness in deriving human laws from the natural law. Such arbitrariness explains why there can be justifiable variation in human laws across time and place, and also why human laws are necessary to supplement the natural law. Human laws are necessary to determine – that is, render more determinate – what the natural law leaves general and open. To take a familiar example, consider a law governing a typical coordination problem, such as the problem of settling on a particular side of the road on which everyone is to drive. Presumably, the natural law is indeterminate with respect to whether we should drive on the right or the left. Both possible solutions to the coordination problem, introduced by the need to have everyone drive on the same side of the road, are consistent with the natural law, but a choice needs to be made. Reason alone does not, and cannot, tell us which side to drive on, though it does tell us that it should be one side or the other. So a choice must be made, to render one of the options salient – the option the natural law requires that we pursue once a human authority (or established custom) has chosen it for us.

In commenting on the two modes of derivation, Aquinas makes this observation:

> Accordingly both modes of derivation are found in the human law. But those things which are derived in the first way, are contained in human law not as emanating therefrom exclusively, but have some force from the natural law also. But those things which are derived in the second way, *have no other force than that of human law.* (Aquinas, 2017, 40; emphasis added)

Unfortunately, Aquinas slips up in the last sentence, which can only be understood as a misstatement (Finnis, 1998, 267). It is of course true that the decision that creates a human law (that we ought to drive on the right side of the road) plays a decisive role in the creation, and therefore force, of the human law. But – and this is crucial – the force of such a human law still requires conformity with the natural law: that harm ought to be avoided, safety and efficiency ought to be pursued, etc. It is remarkable just how often Aquinas's misstatement is missed, so it is worth spelling out the idea in full. The rule "drive on the right side of the road" would conform to and so derive its force from the natural law principles of avoiding harm, pursuing safety, efficiency, etc. Likewise, the rule "drive on the left side of the road" would also conform to, and so derive its force from, the very same natural law principles. In both instances, a human decision (drive on the right or drive on the left) is essential, but in both instances conformity with the natural law is still required to give force to the human law. The nonsense of a human law saying that we ought to drive in the middle of the road clearly shows there are moral limits, imposed by the natural law, on what human laws could justifiably be. So, even when there is choice, it is choice constrained within certain parameters set by the natural law, which ultimately explains the force of all human laws. To say that correctly derived human laws, by way of determination, "have no other force than that of human law" obscures this important point.

1.3 John Finnis

Aquinas's natural law theory has been carefully and meticulously elaborated and developed by John Finnis, though with one important difference. While Aquinas works from within a theological worldview (in the thirteenth century over most of Europe, this was a safe, indeed necessary, commitment), Finnis aims to develop a natural law theory of law and morality free from such a presumption. Finnis supposes we can identify what is good for human beings and societies by relying solely on our nature and capacity as rational beings – beings who can think and reason about what is good for them.

This difference aside, there are important similarities between Aquinas and Finnis. The main similarity is agreement over the purpose of philosophy of law. In Aquinas's philosophical system, everything is to be understood in terms of its purpose or end, and law is no exception. For Aquinas, the purpose of law is the common good, and the basic precept of the natural law is that good ought to be pursued and evil avoided (Aquinas, 2017, 35). Finnis shares these beliefs without reservation and offers a sophisticated account of what the good is. In Finnis's view, there are in fact seven basic human goods: life, knowledge, play, aesthetic experience, friendship, practical reasonableness, and religion (Finnis, 1980, 85–90). These goods are basic, irreducible, exhaustive, incommensurable, objective, universal, self-evident, and known by reason and fact. They also represent the objectives of meaningful, long-standing projects, not momentary, fleeting options. In this sense, they provide the basic values that humans have reason to pursue.

Finnis also shares Aquinas's view that human laws can be derived from what is objectively and universally good for humans. To see how his argument works, we first need to elaborate on one of the basic goods: practical reasonableness.

Practical reasonableness begins with some basic observations about us and our lives – namely, that we cannot pursue fully all of the basic goods in our life, nor are we all equally suited to pursue each and every basic good. It is also important to observe that the basic goods are not presented, on their own, as norms or rules of any kind. How should we then structure our attitudes, dispositions, and actions with respect to them?

As Finnis explains, practical reasonableness is constituted by several principles that are meant to guide our choices, actions, attitudes, and commitments (Finnis, 1980, ch. 5):

(i)   We should structure our life by means of a coherent plan, which takes one or more of the basic goods as the basis of long-term commitment(s).
(ii) We cannot have arbitrary preferences amongst the goods.
(iii) We cannot have arbitrary preferences amongst persons.
(iv) We must be both detached and committed to our projects.
(v)   Consequences and efficiency matter in the assessment of our actions, but they are not of overriding importance.
(vi) We must respect, in every act, every basic good.
(vii) We have a responsibility to promote the common good.
(viii) We must follow our conscience.

The product of these requirements of practical reasonableness, supplemented by their guidance in considering particular issues, is morality, but not just any morality. The requirements and their implications represent the true, objective, universal morality, regardless of how much it might not be recognized or may have been ignored.

Together, the requirements of practical reasonableness offer guidance to individuals about how to live well. Yet they also offer guidance to lawmakers who have the responsibility to devise morally sound laws. Here is an example.[2] Consider the first requirement – that we should structure our life by means of a coherent plan, which takes one or more of the basic goods as the basis of long-term commitment(s). This means that we must not drift without commitment to any of the goods, nor attempt to live according to a blueprint of life where thought and judgment are replaced by mechanical rule-following. Nonetheless, changes to life plans are permissible, so long as they are made thoughtfully and reasonably, with the basic goods in mind. Now, making and following commitments and plans depends – as a kind of precondition – on a fairly stable environment where our expectations enjoy some degree of security. To establish

---

[2] I do not mean to suggest that this example, especially as it is presented here, is a precise reproduction of Finnis's argument. It is, rather, a simplified version of the kind of derivation Finnis presents much more elaborately (Finnis, 1980, 270–73).

and maintain such an environment puts an obligation on governments, and others with power and responsibility, to avoid thwarting or undermining people's expectations. Tracing this line of reasoning, we arrive at an important and familiar part of political morality:[3] the rule of law. Some of the familiar principles of the rule of law, which constrain officials in all of their activities, are that laws must be open, prospective, stable, clear, and consistent (Fuller, 1969, ch. 2; Raz, 2009a, ch. 11). Only with laws that abide by such principles will it be possible (again, as a precondition) for people to make and follow through with their commitments and plans as forms of participation in the basic goods.

This is of course just one example, though I believe others can be offered. We could derive in a similar way, for instance, the political value of liberty or freedom from the second requirement of practical reasonableness, or the political value of equality from the third requirement. It is not my aim to explore such derivations any further, but only to observe the role they play in Finnis's natural law theory: the political values, when correctly derived from the basic human goods, serve as objective, universal, unchanging moral values, and as natural laws, they explain the conditions under which human laws are morally binding or obligatory. In Finnis's words, "the principles of the natural law explain the obligatory force (in the fullest sense of 'obligation') of positive laws" (Finnis, 1980, 23–24).

1.4 Moral Fallibility of Human Laws

As I mentioned, it is not my intention to assess the particular natural law theories of Aristotle, Aquinas, and Finnis, which, despite some key differences, all fall within the same Western and European tradition. For example, compare Finnis's list of seven basic goods with the five basic interests identified in Sharia law: life, religion, reproduction, property, and reason (Emon, 2010). How might we go about arguing whether one or the other list is correct? There are also many Indigenous natural law theories, which have received virtually no attention in Western legal theory and offer quite different understandings of how humans ought to relate to others and the natural world (Williams, 2018). A truly cross-cultural study of natural law theory is important and would be tremendously valuable, but it is well beyond my present scope and purpose. What I do wish to maintain, and endorse, is that in abstracting from the particular claims and starting points of various natural law theories there remains a viable and essential observation: that human, positive laws are answerable, everywhere

---

[3] By "political morality" I mean that kind or part of morality that applies to those with governance responsibilities in their political communities – for example, a legislative assembly in a representative democracy.

and always, to standards of morality that exist apart from and prior to those laws. Put in different terms, to give rise to moral reasons or obligations to act, human laws must respect these standards of morality, whatever their ultimate source or nature. From natural law theory we therefore get this basic commitment: to explain the moral normativity of law requires appeal to moral reasons or values.

I will have more to say about this commitment in Section 8, once all other commitments and dimensions of the normativity of law have been assembled and can be viewed together, but the reader might understandably ask for more by way of defense at this stage. The necessity and importance of an account of law's moral normativity, which requires an investigation into the source of morality that can support the bindingness of law, rests precisely on the fact of law's moral fallibility: human lawmakers can and often do create laws that fail to live up to critical standards of morality. That laws are morally fallible in this way supports the conclusion that, everywhere and always, laws must be scrutinized from a moral point of view. Such scrutiny is essential for understanding the moral dimension to the problem of the normativity of law – that is, the moral reasons we have to follow or obey the law (or not).

2 Classical Legal Positivism: Hobbes, Bentham, Austin

In the last section we saw how natural law theorists, such as Aquinas and Finnis, emphasized the importance of conformity of human, positive law with objective, critical standards of morality. Both emphasized that human laws can fail in this regard, yet insisted that we have the most to learn about the normativity of law by viewing law under conditions of success – that is, where it does conform to, or is correctly derived from, true morality. Attention shifts, however, with the views of early legal positivists, who also recognized that law can fail in its moral justification yet still present such a force in our practical lives through its use of coercive orders that the nature and character of its demands alone warrant sustained theoretical investigation. This section will highlight key elements of the views of those – such as Thomas Hobbes, Jeremy Bentham, and John Austin – who can be labeled "command theorists" of law. Much as in the preceding section, the goal here is not to defend or criticize in any great detail, but to continue to survey and assemble various conceptions of the normativity of law for subsequent reflection.

2.1 Thomas Hobbes

We can begin with a somewhat ambiguous example of a legal positivist. It is difficult to categorize Hobbes (1588–1679) as either a natural law theorist or legal positivist, but thankfully this is not necessary, and, as I shall explain in a moment, it is even valuable not to do so, as Hobbes offers an early example of a pluralist approach to explaining the normativity of law. Hobbes thought there were various natural laws, understood as objective principles of morality, but also noted the crucial fact that human law represents a distinct feature of political society. For Hobbes, effective order in society required an all-powerful sovereign to whom everyone owed obedience, which led him to frame the problem of the normativity of law in a way that still holds today: the challenge of explaining why it would be rational for self-interested persons to subject themselves to a sovereign and accept a general obligation to obey (Rawls, 1971; Simmons, 1979; Smith, 1973). According to Hobbes, the answer was relatively simple: one's self-interest would be better protected living under conditions of sovereign rule than in the absence of such rule, as one might imagine in a state of nature.

This conception of the problem of the normativity of law – what might make it reasonable to comply with law, from the point of view of rational self-interest – is similar to, but also different from, the conception of the problem of normativity of law introduced by natural law theorists. First, the difference: For Hobbes, and certain other social contract theorists (Gauthier, 1986), the problem of the normativity of law was to establish prudential reasons to conform to the law or fulfill one's legal obligations, while for natural law theorists, it was not prudential reasons that gave law its normativity, but moral reasons.[4] So understood, this part Hobbes's account of the normativity of law is *evaluative*, but what we might call *prudentially evaluative*, in contrast to morally evaluative. Next, the similarity: Both Hobbes and the natural law theorists looked outside of positive, enacted law for its objective normative force. Both prudential reasons and moral reasons exist prior to, and independently of, humanly created law and, as such, both can be used as critical standards to assess positive law. The normative force of human law, on both views, crucially rests on something outside of itself.[5]

What is also interesting for our current purposes, however, is another part of Hobbes's account, and this is the attention he pays to the distinct way in which a sovereign attempts to rule – namely, by claiming obedience through the issuing of commands. This attention represents a related, but distinguishable, dimension to understanding the normativity of law, which leads in a different

---

[4] Things of course get complicated if one sees no difference between prudential reasons and moral reasons, or sees one kind (e.g., moral reasons) as derivative from the other (e.g., prudential reasons). We can leave these complications for others.

[5] For a recent account of the normativity of law that places prudential reasons at the center, see Himma, 2020.

investigative direction than looking for external, objective reasons for obeying law. Along this dimension, Hobbes focuses on the unique way in which law makes its demands, and offers this nugget of analysis on the concept of "command": "Command is, where a man saith, *Doe this*, or *Doe not this*, without expecting other reason than the Will of him that sayes it" (Hobbes, 1985, 303). The idea here is now a familiar one: that a central part of the claim to authority, especially political authority to create and impose law, takes the form of "do this because I said so." Hobbes is here distinguishing the idea of command from the idea of counsel, with one mark of the distinction lying in whose benefit is targeted: "Therefore between Counsell and Command, one great difference is, that Command is directed to a mans own benefit; and Counsell to the benefit of another man" (Hobbes, 1985, 303). Hobbes thought it was true by definition that a command must be understood always as directed at the commander's own benefit, but we can set this claim aside. The next difference is more interesting: "And from this ariseth another difference, that a man may be obliged to do what he is Commanded; as when he hath coven-anted to obey: But he cannot be obliged to do as he is Counselled, because the hurt of not following it, is his own; or if he should covenant to follow it, then is the Counsell turned into the nature of a Command" (Hobbes, 1985, 303). We need not follow all of Hobbes's reasoning here, though it is important to see what he is doing: he is building an argument to show the precise way in which commands are a structurally distinctive kind of normative phenomena, of the kind that purport to give rise to obligations. This is crucial for explanation of the conceptual or descriptive–explanatory dimension of the normativity of law, for as Hobbes later claims, "it is manifest, that Law in generall, is not Counsell, but Command" (Hobbes, 1985, 312). Pinpointing the exact way in which law presents itself, or asserts itself, is definitive of how some later theorists would come to see an important part of the problem of the normativity of law (see Sections 3 and 4).

2.2 Jeremy Bentham and John Austin

The notion of command of course forms the backbone of the legal positivist theories of Jeremy Bentham and John Austin in the eighteenth and nineteenth centuries. Unlike Hobbes, both Bentham and Austin rejected natural law theory, especially its key claims that (i) there are natural principles of morality out there, or natural rights, accessible to everyone to discover by means of their natural capacity for rational reflection (Bentham, 1987, 53); and (ii) explanation and understanding of the existence and character of legal obligation required seeing true, genuine legal obligations as conforming with those objective principles of morality. Austin, for example, had no sympathy for the view that immoral or unjust laws were not really laws or did not give rise to real obligations if they violated some objective natural or moral order laid down by God:

> Suppose an act innocuous, or positively beneficial, be prohibited by the sovereign under the penalty of death; if I commit this act, I shall be tried and condemned, and if I object to the sentence, that it is contrary to the law of God, who has commanded that human lawgivers shall not prohibit acts which have no evil consequences, the Court of Justice will demonstrate the inconclusiveness of my reasoning by hanging me up, in pursuance of the law of which I have impugned the validity. (Austin, 2000, 185)

According to Bentham and Austin, the normativity of law was to be understood in terms of socially observable facts, and the key social facts to observe – that is, the essential social patterns of behavior to observe – were relations of superiors and inferiors.[6] Such relations of superiors and inferiors were best exhibited in the effective issuance of commands, so for Bentham and Austin commands were the constitutive social facts of law. As Austin defined it, a command is "1. A wish or desire conceived by a rational being, that another rational being shall do or forbear. 2. An evil to proceed from the former, and to be incurred by the latter, in case the latter comply not with the wish. 3. An expression or intimation of the wish by words or other signs" (Austin, 2000, 17). Turning to law, according to Austin a law is to be understood as a species of command: a law is a general command or standing order to do or not do something, and to be under a legal obligation is to be subject to penalty or punishment if one does not comply with a general command by the sovereign. So, expressed in different terms, the core idea in Austin's and Bentham's "Command Theory of Law" is coercion, but coercion used through the means of standing commands or orders: where law exists, conduct is nonoptional and obligatory because its demand is backed by the threat of the use of force.[7] This last observation, for Bentham and Austin, was the key to explaining the normativity of law, as it marked the

---

[6] Later legal positivists turned away from coercive relationships as the key to understanding law and instead viewed the general practices of coordination among officials (i.e., judges, legislators, police) as paramount to explanation of the nature of law.

[7] There is an important nuance to Bentham's view, which ought to be noted and is well put by Fred Schauer:

> Bentham's focus on coercion as lying at the heart of law was ... based on his empirical psychological assessment that other-regarding and social-regarding interests would rarely (but, it should be emphasized again, not never) be sufficient to motivate people to put aside their self-regarding motivations. To the extent that law seeks to promote the common good at the expense of individual preferences and interests, therefore, its ability to threaten or impose unpleasant sanctions emerges for Bentham as the principal way in which it can accomplish this end. More importantly, the threat of sanctions is for

distinctive way in which law presents itself and claims an impact on our normative lives.[8]

We ought to note, however, that while both Bentham and Austin rejected some key claims in natural law theory, they did not reject the idea that there was an objective standard of morality for laws to live up to, and which could be used precisely as a critical standard to assess laws. While Bentham's account was far more elaborate, both Bentham and Austin were utilitarians and saw the principle of utility as key to moral assessment of good and bad laws. While there were exceptions, the principle of utility was to be used to determine whether there were genuine moral obligations to follow laws, or whether laws needed to be reformed to be more just. It was important to identify laws that failed to meet the principle of utility, as this was relevant to subjects' moral obligations and officials' moral responsibilities – two key perspectives for thinking about the normativity of law.

We have, then, in Bentham's and Austin's work a pluralist approach to the normativity of law similar to that seen in Hobbes. Their analyses struck different balances, but in each instance we see at least two different dimensions, or aspects, of the problem of the normativity of law: one is the evaluative dimension – to investigate the reasons why law might be morally binding or not, or provide prudential reasons to comply or not; and the other is the conceptual or descriptive–explanatory dimension – to accurately depict the characteristic way in which law makes its demands. These dimensions are related, of course, but once again they are separable types of investigation. Recognition of this plurality also helps us to see how Austin's statement in the passage quoted above is misguided as a criticism of natural law theory – a mistake well pointed out by Finnis: "Someone who asks how injustice affects his obligation to conform to law is not likely to be asking for information on the practically important but theoretically banal point of fact, 'Am I or am I not likely to be hanged for non-compliance with this law?'" (Finnis, 1980, 355). Finnis adds:

> It is not conducive to clear thought, or to any good practical purpose, to smudge the positivity of law by denying the legal obligatoriness *in the legal or intra-systemic sense* of a rule recently affirmed as legally valid and obligatory by the highest institution of the "legal system." (Austin's concern to make this point, in the "hanging me up" passage, was quite reasonable.

Bentham sometimes less a part of the *definition* of law than it is law's most prevalent modality and most pervasive characteristic. Coercion is something *added* to legal commands to make them effective by furnishing supplemental motives for compliance. (Schauer, 2015, 14)

[8] This was important for both Bentham and Austin, since both wished to emphasize law's coercive power as a means of putting us on alert to the need for moral justification of political authority and potential reform of laws should they prove wanting (Schauer, 2015, ch. 2).

What was unreasonable was his failure to acknowledge ... the existence of questions which may be expressed in the same language but which are not determinately answerable intra-systemically.) (Finnis, 1980, 357)

Here, Finnis is pointing to the different senses in which we might ask about law's obligatoriness or normativity: one is intrasystemic (i.e., conceptual or descriptive–explanatory), the sense in which law claims and demonstrates its force; the other is distinctly moral (i.e., morally evaluative) and asks about law's moral as opposed to its institutional or intrasystemic force. I believe Finnis is correct on this score. Considered holistically, it is best to see that Austin's view exhibited pluralism, as he recognized both (i) that as a descriptive–explanatory matter law characteristically claims force to do its job, and (ii) that as a morally evaluative matter law must also answer to an objective standard of morality to be morally binding (the principle of utility, which Austin understood as an index to God's will [Austin, 2000, 73]). The "hanging me up" passage is therefore best rejected as mistaken in purpose and aim; it was a missed opportunity to make plain the possibility and necessity of a pluralist approach to understanding law's normativity (Schauer, 2015, 18).

To avoid misunderstanding, I do not want to give the impression that with each difference in how the problem of the normativity of law is conceived we have simply addition and never disagreement. It is well known that command theories of law came under sustained attack by H. L. A. Hart in the twentieth century. In Hart's most influential book, *The Concept of Law*, he focused his criticism on Austin's version of the command theory, and showed precisely why the notions of threats, habits of obedience, and sovereigns could not form the basis of a general jurisprudence about the nature and character of law, for these simply left out or distorted too many familiar instances of law. I will return to Hart's criticisms and more recent debates about the relation between law and coercion in Section 7. There, I will argue that while Hart was partially correct in his criticisms of Austin, he is also responsible for a false and unfortunate dichotomy in how the relation has come to be understood, especially as it bears on questions of the normativity of law.

3 Twentieth-Century Positivism: Kelsen and Hart

Legal positivists in the twentieth century continued to work on isolating the problem of the normativity of law from a descriptive–explanatory or conceptual perspective, but not with the belief that commands or coercion formed an essential part of the explanation. Focus turned instead to how legal normativity was possible, and itself a category distinct from other types of normativity, as well as how legal normativity had a self-image as a special kind of reason for action. This section will present these ideas through the work of perhaps the two most influential legal positivists of the twentieth century: Hans Kelsen and H. L. A. Hart.

3.1 Hans Kelsen

Kelsen agreed with earlier positivists that part of the explanation of the normativity of law required recognition that positive laws were acts of will, but insisted that acts of will alone could not explain the normativity of law for categorical reasons:

> "Norm" is the meaning of an act by which a certain behavior is commanded, permitted, or authorized. The norm, as the specific meaning of an act directed toward the behavior of someone else, is to be carefully differentiated from the act of will whose meaning the norm is: the norm is an *ought*, but the act of will is an *is*. Hence the situation constituted by such an act must be described by the statement: The one individual wills that the other individual ought to behave in a certain way. The first part of this sentence refers to an *is*, the existing fact of the first individual's act of volition; the second part to an *ought*, to a norm as the meaning of that act. Therefore it is incorrect to assert – as is often done – that the statement: "An individual ought" merely means that another individual wills something; that the *ought* can be reduced to an *is*." (Kelsen, 1970, 5)

The normativity of law was something quite special, Kelsen thought, and could not be reduced to an account of facts, such as acts of will, as Hobbes, Bentham, and Austin supposed. However, as a positivist, Kelsen did not think that explanation of the normativity of law rested on an account of morality, or any other source, beyond law itself. A theory of law, to do its job properly, had to be "pure":

> It is called a "pure" theory of law, because it only describes the law and attempts to eliminate from the object of this description everything that is strictly not law: its aim is to free the science of law from alien elements . . . Such an approach seems a matter of course. Yet, a glance upon the traditional science of law as it developed during the nineteenth and twentieth centuries clearly shows how far removed it is from the postulate of purity; uncritically the science of law has been mixed with elements of psychology, sociology, ethics, and political theory. (Kelsen, 1970, 1)

When Kelsen sets out to identify the special and distinctive nature of law, he means it. Law, for Kelsen, has a unique nature, and its normativity is to be explained through development of the idea of legal validity. Legal validity is neither moral validity, which can be understood as conformity with standards of morality, nor logical validity, which can be understood as satisfaction of the rules of inference and derivation. Instead, legal validity refers to a special mode of existence of norms, which exist as commanded, permitted, or authorized within a special kind of institutional system, a legal system. Legal validity is also, to repeat, a normative phenomenon, a distinct kind of oughtness. The problem of the normativity of law, in Kelsen's view, was to explain precisely how norms exist as legally valid, with the nature of legal oughtness.

Since norms, as oughts, could not be reduced to facts, their source (and explanation) could only be other norms or oughts. This led Kelsen to his famous view that legal norms must always be structured and organized as systems of norms, with a basic norm serving as the ultimate foundation (and providing for the reason of validity) of all the other norms in the legal system. Again, validation in this legal sense is different from moral validation or logical validation (i.e., there could be legally valid norms which were immoral from a moral point of view, or connected to higher norms, not by deduction, implication, or inference, but simply because they have been created in a way commanded, authorized, or permitted by those higher norms). But what explained the normativity of the basic norm? Here, Kelsen insisted that it could not be grounded in any account of facts, such as acts of will, but simply had to be presumed, for only norms can bestow normativity on other norms: "Since the reason for the validity of a norm can only be another norm, the presupposition must be a norm: not one posited (i.e., created) by a legal authority, but a presupposed norm . . ." (Kelsen, 1970, 200). The presupposition of the basic norm was also necessary, Kelsen believed, to bring an end to an otherwise infinite regress:

> The norm which represents the reason for the validity of another norm is called, as we have said, the "higher" norm. But the search for the reason of a norm's validity cannot go on indefinitely like the search for the cause of an effect. It must end with a norm which, as the last and highest, is presupposed. (Kelsen, 1970, 194)

Focusing on the legal validity of constitutions, which typically purport to validate all other norms of a legal system, Kelsen explains:

> If we ask for the reason of the validity of the constitution, that is, for the reason of the validity of the norms regulating the creation of the general norms, we may, perhaps, discover an older constitution; that means the validity of the existing constitution is justified by the fact that it was created according to the rules of an earlier constitution by way of a constitutional amendment. In this way we eventually arrive at a historically first constitution that cannot have been created in this way and whose validity, therefore, cannot be traced back to a positive norm created by a legal authority; . . . If we ask for the reason of the validity of the historically first constitution, then

the answer can only be . . . that the validity of this constitution – the assumption that it is a binding norm – must be presupposed . . . (Kelsen, 1970, 200)

Kelsen also arrived at the view that for there to be law across the world, it all had
to be unified, in some way, with a single basic norm validating all international
and national laws under a single legal system. This dimension of his view need
not concern us here, for the basic elements of his understanding of – and answer
to – the problem of the normativity of law are in place: law consists of a special,
unique category of normative thought, which has as a central feature the idea
(or mode of existence) of legal validity, which is *sui generis* (i.e., distinct from
moral validity, logical validity, sociological validity, political validity, etc.)
Alternatively put, Kelsen's conception of the problem of the normativity of
law is to be understood as a question about the possibility and ultimate foundation of legal normativity as a distinct type of normativity.

3.2 H. L. A. Hart

A comparison between Hart and Kelsen reveals similarities and differences.
Among the similarities, and in Hart's own words, "I share with [Kelsen] the
conviction that a central task of legal philosophy is to explain the normative
force of propositions of law which figure both in academic legal writing and in
the discourse of judges and lawyers" (Hart, 1983, 18). Hart also believed, along
with Kelsen, that to explain the nature of law required understanding law's
special existence in institutionalized normative systems, and devoted much
attention to explaining the notion of legal validity and the associated idea of
legal system. For Hart, like Kelsen, legal validity was to be distinguished from
both moral validity and logical validity. Legal validity was also to be understood
as a special character of legal norms, explained in terms of their mode of
existence rather than their content.[9]

There are two important differences between Hart's and Kelsen's views. The
first is that while Kelsen's "pure theory of law," by design, saw no room for
sociological or psychological elements to form part of an explanation of the
nature or normativity of law, Hart gave such elements a rather central place. In
one sense, Hart's "rule of recognition" – the ultimate rule of any legal system,
and which determines the criteria of validity for all norms of the system –
appears much like a socialized or psychologized version of Kelsen's basic
norm. The rule of recognition, as Hart presents it, is a thoroughly social rule,
which requires for its elucidation understanding of sociological elements of

---

[9] Here, I leave to the side the issue that Hart appears to accept that, under certain conditions, moral
   criteria could be included among the ultimate criteria of legal validity in some legal system. See
   Waluchow, 1994.

patterns of behavior and collective social pressure, and psychological elements of internalization, acceptance, and a critical normative attitude (Hart, 2012, chs. 4–6). As a social fact theory of law, Hart's view required no less than a proper understanding of the kinds of social facts upon which law rests and operates.[10]

A second key difference – and one more crucial to identify for the purposes of this Element, though it might best be described as a crystallization and emphasis of certain aspects of Kelsen's view – is the focus on law's special place and role in practical reasoning. As Hart understood things, the problem of the normativity of law was one of explaining the way in which law could be seen to constitute "a reason for action of a special kind" (Hart, 1982, 243). In "Commands and Authoritative Reasons," Hart revisits some of the problems he saw with Bentham's (and Austin's) command theories of law, but develops an idea he thought they had correctly sensed: the idea of an authoritative reason (Hart, 1982, ch. X). To build up to the idea of an authoritative reason, Hart introduces[11] the idea of a "content-independent reason." Using the notion of a command as an example (other examples are promises and social rules), Hart explains:

> Content-independence of commands lies in the fact that a commander may issue many different commands to the same or to different people and the actions commanded may have nothing in common, yet in the case of all of them the commander intends his expressions of intention to be taken as a reason for doing them. It is therefore intended to function as a reason independently of the nature or character of the actions to be done. (Hart, 1982, 254)

The idea of a command – as a reason for action on its own – is in turn explained as a "peremptory" reason for action, where the expression of the command is meant to take the place of other reasons, and deliberation, for the subject. This much the command theory of law had right, but as Hart goes on to argue, the abstracted features of content-independence and peremptory reasons for action have much greater explanatory power and serve to show how other kinds of law and legal practices, which do not take the form or character of commands, are best understood. General recognition in society of law-creating and dispute-resolving powers, as well as private powers of contract, are all best explained as the use and exhibition of content-independent, peremptory reasons (e.g., the legislature so enacted, the court so decided, the parties so agreed, etc.).[12]

---

[10] Some have criticized Hart's theory for not being social or sociological enough: Tamanaha, 2001; Twining, 2009; Cotterrell, 2017.

[11] Strictly speaking, in discussing the idea of a promise Hart first coined the expression "independence of content" in "Legal and Moral Obligation" (Hart, 1958).

[12] "What is crucial for legislation is that certain things said or done by certain persons which can be construed as guiding actions should be recognized by the Courts as constituting just such peremptory reasons for action, and so as law-making events" (Hart, 1982, 260).

Insistence on the content-independent, peremptory nature of legal obligations and norms also goes hand in hand with Hart's positivist view on the conceptual separation of law and morality. Once it is recognized that there is a disconnection between the fact that a rule giving rise to a legal obligation has been created (its content-independence) and whatever that rule might require (its content), it becomes quite easy to see that the content of a rule could be directed towards a just or unjust action, or moral or immoral conduct. On this, Hart and Kelsen agreed.

Though they give different answers, there is nonetheless an important overlap in how Kelsen and Hart framed their conceptions of the problem of the normativity of law, which include two related aspects: a question about the ultimate foundation of law (how legal validity or legal "oughtness" comes to exist in the first place), and a question about the special character of reasoning according to law (i.e., how legal reasoning is distinctive). These are related in the following way: the identification of a legal norm (i.e., pointing to legal normativity) is carried out by tracing its validity through authorizing or recognition rules until one arrives at an ultimate source in the form of a basic norm or rule of recognition. Legal normativity, we can also say, is detected by locating this type of source-based reasoning, where one appeals to the legal validity of norms as the basis for claims about legal obligations, legal rights, legal permissions, etc. What both saw quite clearly is that a special form of reasoning can emerge with the creation of legal sources, which serve as points of reference (or recognition, in Hart's words).

A remaining difference, however, is what both see and understand at the foundation of law. For Kelsen, legal normativity can only bottom out in legal normativity, or a highest norm. Otherwise, there is no legal normativity at any level. For Hart, it was important to observe that at the foundations of law was nothing more than a socio-psychological recognition of authority; in essence, legal authority is created (invented) by social practice, and nothing more:

> It may, as in the early law of many societies, be no more than that an authoritative list or text of the rules is to be found in a written document or carved on some public monument. No doubt as a matter of history this step from the pre-legal to the legal may be accomplished in distinguishable stages, of which the first is the mere reduction to writing of hitherto unwritten rules. This is not itself the crucial step, though it is a very important one: *what is crucial is the acknowledgement of reference to the writing or inscription as authoritative, i.e. as the proper way of disposing of doubts as to the existence of the rule.* (Hart, 2012, 94–95; emphasis added)

For some reason, many see this as a failure on Hart's part to explain how law can be normative: How can law be normative if at its foundation there is nothing more than some kind of social acceptance or recognition?[13] But this is a rather odd kind of accusation against Hart, for it was precisely his point – as a legal positivist concerned to show that nothing follows about what we ought to do given the existence of law – to show that at the foundations of law was nothing more than the fact of social acceptance. This is likely not a failure, but a sober reminder about law. It is also a lesson most forcefully explained and defended by Joseph Raz, as we will see in Section 4.

4 Twentieth-Century Positivism: Raz

Among the major figures in English-speaking jurisprudence in the twentieth century, it is fairly safe to say that none advanced our understanding of law as a form of practical reason as much as Joseph Raz. This section will lay out some of the core elements of Raz's view and show that, while he did not present his account as pluralist, it displays the pluralism identified in preceding sections in its clearest form. In Raz's framework there are both conceptual and morally evaluative tasks to understanding the normativity of law.

4.1 Reasons for Action

Raz once described the philosophy of law as a branch of practical philosophy (Raz, 1999, 11), which has the idea of a reason for action at its center. Reasons for action are values, desires, interests, principles, etc., which count in favor of doing or not doing something. "To stay dry," for example, is a reason for taking an umbrella outside if it is raining. "To save money" is a reason for waiting for a sale before buying a new television. "To remain awake" is a reason for drinking coffee before watching your child's baseball game. Reasons for action, Raz adds, also exist at different levels, depending on the role they play in practical reasoning. First-order or operative reasons are those reasons that play a role in explaining and justifying what ultimately counts in favor of some course of action. They are justifying reasons, one could say, and are described as first-order reasons by Raz since they are reasons that ultimately provide reasons in favor of, or counting towards, some particular course of action.[14] They are also first-order reasons since they typically constitute deliberation absent any decisions, rules, directives, or other general devices we might use as shortcuts or alternatives to deliberation. Decisions, rules, and directives, in Raz's view, are understood as second-order reasons.

---

[13] See discussion in Section 6.
[14] Raz also describes operative reasons as those reasons which provide a critical practical attitude towards conduct (Raz, 1999, 32–33).

Consider an example. In deciding whether or not to take an umbrella, I can deliberate about and weigh several first-order, operative reasons, though perhaps identification of just two will suffice for our purposes here: staying dry and avoiding the inconvenience of having to carry an umbrella around. (In addition to these reasons, I will of course also need to make some guesses about the chances and amount of rain I might face while I am out.) But there are also second-order reasons, such as settled habits or rules of thumb, or directives, that I might adopt or follow instead. These might include the settled habit or rule of thumb of always taking an umbrella with me whenever I leave the house, just in case, or a watchful parent or partner instructing me to take an umbrella as I prepare to go out. Settled habits, rules of thumb, and directives can themselves constitute a reason for action, though they are second-order reasons for action. Why "second-order"? Because they are meant to replace, in a sense, the first-order reasons by giving us new reasons that are meant to reflect those first-order reasons but require no appeal to them. Rather than appeal to the first-order reasons about whether or not to take an umbrella, we can rely on the second-order reasons provided by settled habits, rules of thumb, or directives.

This is of course a very brief and selective summary of much more complex argument and analysis, but I believe it will serve well enough. The next question is to ask how this account figures in understanding law. As we will see, it figures quite prominently, as law is also constituted by rules, directives, and decisions, though with one important difference. While "staying dry," "saving money," etc. are easily understood as self-regarding or prudential reasons (for the most part), the typical sorts of first-order reasons that law is meant to reflect, as a form of second-order reason, include other-regarding reasons – namely, moral reasons. The relation between law, practical reason, and morality is intricately explained by Raz, and the resulting view has become foundational in understanding the normativity of law over the last fifty years.

4.2 Law as Practical Reason

Raz's views on the nature and normativity of law are rich and wide-ranging, which makes it difficult to know where to begin. One point of departure would be to frame a key question to which Raz's views provide an answer: What does the law require or demand of its subjects? Notice that this question does not ask about how citizens actually do regard or treat the law, or what they actually think of it. For Raz, these would be empirical or sociological questions, whose answers would in all likelihood display very little uniformity. They are also questions that fall squarely outside the bounds of the philosophy of law. Instead, Raz's central concern is to explain the character of law's self-image: how law presents itself, or conceives of itself, to subjects.[15] The answer, which we will unpack, is that law claims moral authority; it claims to govern subjects by settling for them what they ought to do, morally speaking.

What is the evidence for the view that law claims authority? Here, Raz points to some phenomena, from which we are to draw some conceptual abstractions:

> The claims the law makes for itself are evident from the language it adopts and from the opinions expressed by its spokesmen, i.e. by the institutions of the law. The law's claim to authority is manifested by the fact that legal institutions are officially designated as "authorities," by the fact that they regard themselves as having the right to impose obligations on their subjects, by their claims that their subjects owe them allegiance, and that their subjects ought to obey the law as it requires to be obeyed … (Raz, 1995, 215–16)

We might wish for more evidence, or more of an argument, for this important part of Raz's view or why he thinks, rather than merely assumes, that it is necessarily *moral* authority that is claimed (Raz, 1995, 215). Nonetheless, it is rather easy to find examples that display the kinds of claims he has in mind. For example, those driving along the Don Valley Parkway, connecting northern and southern parts of the city of Toronto, will often see this statement on the electronic signs above: "Hands-free devices only while driving. It's the law!" Part of the criminal law in Canada includes this offense: "It is an offense to willfully promote hatred, other than in private conversation, toward any section of the public distinguished by color, race, religion, or ethnic origin." And perhaps most succinctly, the all-too-familiar red octagonal sign "Stop." Each of these laws, made by the relevant authorities, can be understood as demands for obedience, as obligations citizens are expected and bound to follow.

But it is how these laws demand obedience, or claim authority over their subjects, that Raz highlights as particularly important. Building on the picture from Section 3, the law claims to serve as a special reason for action for its subjects: it claims legitimate moral authority over its subjects by settling for them what they ought to do. To explain the idea of a claim to legitimate authority, Raz introduces three core theses:

(i) *Dependence Thesis*: "All authoritative directives should be based, among other factors, on reasons which apply to the subjects of those directives and which bear on the circumstances covered by the directives. Such reasons I shall call dependent reasons" (Raz, 1995, 214). (We can note that the idea of dependent reasons here corresponds to the idea of operative reasons explained earlier.) For example, for tax laws to be legitimate, they ought to be based on

---

[15] Raz acknowledges this kind of personification in Raz, 2009b, 38.

reasons of fairness, justice, mutual benefit. Traffic laws should be based on reasons of safety and efficiency. So, according to this first thesis, for law's claims to be legitimate, they must be based on the reasons subjects have that are relevant to the particular area of practical life (e.g., taxation, traffic, etc.).

(ii) *Normal Justification Thesis*: The normal way to justify a person's or law's authority is to show that subjects are better off (i.e., more likely to act as they should according to reason) if they follow that person or law than if they tried to figure out for themselves what the first-order or dependent reasons require them to do (Raz, 1995, 214). The two main ways in which laws are normally justified is by appeal to expertise or coordination, where it is better to follow someone else's directive or behave according to an established coordination convention (again, think of traffic laws).

(iii) *Preemption Thesis*: Laws are special kinds of preemptive or exclusionary reasons; they are meant to reflect and replace (by preempting or excluding appeal to) dependent reasons (Raz, 1995, 214). For example, the law represented by a "Stop" sign does not ask us to think about safety and efficiency on each occasion, but is meant to serve as a new, decisive, or conclusive reason in their place. The "Stop" sign simply tells us to stop, as an all-things-considered directive.[16]

What is essential to understand about the three theses is that together they represent the truth or legitimacy conditions of law's claim to moral authority. They are guides to moral evaluation, and tell us how we are to judge that law's claims to legitimate authority are in fact true or justified claims. (The three theses also apply broadly to particular laws, areas of law, legal systems, officials, and institutions.) In turn, when a law's claim to authority is legitimate, citizens have a moral (and not just a legal) obligation to obey – that is, to treat the law as their preemptive reason for action.[17]

4.3 Preconditions of Law's Authority

Raz also explains the Dependence, Normal Justification, and Preemption theses as amounting to what he calls the "service conception" of law's authority. The idea is that by reflecting and replacing appeal to first-order, dependent reasons, which sometimes might fail to point to a single conclusion, the law provides a service to its subjects. Instead of deliberating about safety and efficiency, and negotiating such deliberations with others engaged in similar deliberations at

---

[16] For example, the legal directive "Stop" presents itself as a special reason for action (it's special because it's meant both (i) to represent the balance of underlying reasons of safety, coordination, clarity, etc. and (ii) to exclude appeal to those underlying reasons).

[17] One complication I will leave aside: the legitimacy of law's claims to moral authority is neither absolute under all circumstances nor uniform for all persons.

each intersection, the "Stop" sign settles our obligations for us. As Raz points out, however, even before we can get to thinking about the moral conditions under which law's claim to legitimate authority is true or justified, it must first be possible for law to claim authority. This calls for an account, of a conceptual or descriptive–explanatory kind, of what we might call the preconditions of law's claim to authority, and as Raz's explains, these are, unlike the three legitimacy theses, of a nonmoral nature.

There are two nonmoral preconditions of law's claim to authority. First, a law must be (or at least be presented as) someone's view about what citizens ought to do. Second, it must be possible to identify the law without having to consider its dependent or underlying reasons. To explain these preconditions, Raz uses an analogy of an arbitrator (Raz, 1995, 212). Suppose A and B refer their dispute (e.g., over the fairness of a contract of employment) to an arbitrator, and the arbitrator returns the following decision: "I have reached the uniquely correct decision. It is the fair decision (i.e., the decision that is uniquely determined by the balance of the reasons of fairness)." Notice that it might be true that the arbitrator has arrived at the uniquely correct decision, but unless they present it to A and B, they have provided no service or solution to A and B, but merely pointed them back to the dependent reason of fairness. A and B, in other words, must be able to identify what the decision is, which requires its presentation or communication by the arbitrator, in a way that does not require appealing to the first-order or dependent reasons that the decision was meant to reflect and replace. Traffic laws that simply told us to "drive safely" or "drive in a coordinated way," tax laws that simply told us to pay "a fair and reasonable amount," and criminal laws that simply told us to "behave morally toward each other" would be similarly defective.

In Raz's view, the fact that law claims authority, which means that it must be capable of having authority, has important implications for testing competing theories of law. In particular, it is well known that Raz argues that inclusive legal positivism – the view that sometimes moral criteria can be among the ultimate validity conditions of law in some legal system – and Dworkin's conception of law as integrity – which holds that law is constituted, and to be identified by, a combination of its social sources and the best moral theory of those social sources (i.e., the best account of their underlying moral reasons) – must both be mistaken, since both suppose that law is to be identified sometimes (inclusive legal positivism) or always (law as integrity) by appealing to moral considerations. Appeal to moral considerations, as Raz maintains, is incompatible with law's claim to authority, and so both of these competing theories fail to fit the facts, so to speak. The view that is compatible with the fact of law's claim to authority, which Raz endorses, is exclusive legal positivism, which maintains that the existence and validity of law must always and everywhere be determined by reference to social sources alone, and never moral considerations. In other words, for law to do what law does (claim authority), and be what law is (a claim to authority), it must be identifiable by recourse to social sources alone, and not require moral evaluation.

4.4 A Pluralist Division of Labor

It is not my aim to assess Raz's view in its particulars – namely, by challenging the way he has characterized the legitimacy conditions of law's authority, or the precise way in which he thinks law claims to offer preemptive or exclusionary reasons for action. But I do wish to remark on and endorse as a key example of pluralism about the normativity of law the structural division of labor he identifies. Let me explain.

Raz's explanation of law's claim to authority, composed of the three moral theses and two nonmoral preconditions identified above, illustrate in an important way how to dissolve a good deal of the so-called dispute between natural law theorists, who insist that law must be understood in terms of its moral purpose, and some legal positivists, who deny any conceptual or necessary connection between law and morality. This is so for two complementary reasons. First, Raz's theory of law's authority maintains, in agreement with natural law theorists such as Aquinas and Finnis, that law must be understood in terms of its moral purpose: in conceiving of law, everywhere and always, one must understand that necessarily law claims *moral* authority to settle for subjects how they ought to conduct themselves. This theoretical commitment is meant to be achieved through conceptual or descriptive–explanatory investigation. In turn, to know when law's moral claims are actually true or justified – itself a crucial part of understanding the normativity of law – requires moral evaluation. Though natural law theorists emphasized each of these points differently, they nonetheless agreed on them. Second, by emphasizing the special significance of law's *claim* for itself to be a moral authority, rather than emphasizing the truth or falsity of such a claim in any or all circumstances, Raz's theory preserves the positivist insistence that particular laws and legal systems everywhere are morally fallible. The very nature of the claim itself is theoretically interesting (as a type of exclusionary reason), for if Raz is right in his explanation (and, again, I am making no claim one way or the other on this), he has shown how to decide between rival theories about the ultimate existence and validity conditions of law. Most importantly, the gap between the nature of the claims law makes, and what might make those claims true, reveals related but still distinct projects for legal theory, one descriptive–explanatory and the other morally evaluative. This division of labor, or pluralistic approach, should come as no surprise. The normativity of law is interesting, important, and significant for several reasons; its theoretical and practical study, to be apt, must also to be multifaceted.

4.5 Taking Stock

Raz's view exhibits the kind of pluralism I believe exists and ought to be preserved in investigations into the normativity of law. Law has a special kind of social existence, characterized by the membership of legal norms in legal systems and their special claims on our practical reason, yet there still remains the additional assessment of law's moral justification to determine whether such claims are true. This pluralist framework is visible in the views of Aquinas and Finnis, who both thought human positive law enjoys its own existence and plays a special role in explaining the normativity of law yet must also be evaluated against the standards of morality. And all agreed, once again, that norms could be legally valid according to the criteria of some actual legal system yet fail to be morally sound. (On this score, I would argue that Raz's "argument from authority," which he deploys against inclusive legal positivism and Dworkin's law as integrity, does not rule out natural law theory. But that is an argument for another day.)

The classical legal positivists – Hobbes, Bentham, and Austin – also agreed that law's social existence was significant, though they emphasized its coercive nature as its most important social character. Exhibiting pluralism as well, they observed that law's moral obligatoriness (or, for Hobbes, its prudential pull) rested on reasons and standards outside positive law itself. Each of these types of investigation, again, forms part of a complete understanding of the normativity of law.

For Kelsen and Hart, the questions of law's normativity also divided between questions about law's moral force and its characteristic mode of existence, as each attempted to explain precisely what is special in identifying norms as distinctly legal norms and not some other kind of norm. They both saw the key to this explanation as lying in an account of the possibility and ultimate foundations of law, again, as a unique kind of institutionalized system of norms. In other words, if Kelsen and Hart are right that law presents a special kind of normative space, of ought-talk and ought-thought, expressed in a distinct form of reasoning according to law (i.e., source-based reasoning), then understanding the foundations of such a normative space is surely part of the problem of understanding the normativity of law.

I mention these various types of questions about the normativity of law – different conceptions of what the problem is – not to suggest that there can be no disagreements between them, but to show that each represents a plausible (and indeed) necessary type of investigation. There has been and will continue to be disagreement about the best way to explain the way law, as a matter of social fact, presents itself to subjects, as well as disagreement about the source and nature of those moral values or principles which, if there are any, do actually justify law's claim to authority (in Raz's terms) or demonstrate law's conformity with universal, objective morality (in Aquinas's and Finnis's terms). Yet there is agreement that law's social existence is on its own a matter of interest worthy of explanation, and there is agreement that law's moral justification is a matter of interest as well, worthy of investigation.

It is worth noting that none of the major figures surveyed so far ever styled themselves as pluralists. But that is beside the point, as I believe their views perform the pluralism and, presented together with attention to similarities and differences, make the pluralist interpretation and value of their work on the normativity of law apparent.

PART II

5 "Third" Theories of Law

This section examines two prominent attempts to overcome the debate between natural law theorists and legal positivists, though in each instance they can be described as fundamentally antipositivist theories, since they are both morally evaluative in aim and purpose. Their views differ, however, from the classical natural law theories of Aquinas and Finnis in supposing that the morality that is relevant for understanding law is not somehow external, standing outside law, but is somehow connected to law internally. In Ronald Dworkin's theory of law as integrity, the relevant morality is to be found in substantive principles that best explain and justify existing legal decisions (legislative and judicial), while in Lon Fuller's procedural natural law theory the relevant morality is a set of formal principles whose observance is believed to yield substantively morally sound laws. In similar but different ways, both Dworkin and Fuller place great weight on law's actual social creation and existence in theorizing its nature and normativity – an emphasis shared with legal positivists. For this reason we can describe their views as "third" theories, as alternatives to both natural law theory and legal positivism.[18] However, as I shall suggest, in trying to find such an alternative space, both fail to heed the lessons of natural law theory and legal positivism demonstrated in Part I: in offering morally evaluative theories, both try to derive too much moral force from the existence of law alone.

---

[18] I am of course following John Mackie's lead, who first referred to Dworkin's theory as a "third theory of law" (Mackie, 1977).

5.1 Law as Integrity

At the outset of Dworkin's work in the philosophy of law, he acknowledges, as natural law theorists and legal positivists do as well, what we can call the moral significance of law – namely, that law has an impact on people's lives and well-being, which makes law, necessarily (Green, 2008), an apt subject matter of moral scrutiny everywhere and always. For example, at the beginning of his influential "The Model of Rules I," he writes:

> Day in and day out we send people to jail, or take money away from them, or make them do things they do not want to do, under coercion of force, and we justify all of this as speaking of such persons as having broken the law or having failed to meet their legal obligations, or having interfered with other people's legal rights ... We may feel confident that what we are doing is proper, but until we can identify the principles we are following we cannot be sure that they are sufficient, or whether we are applying them consistently. (Dworkin, 1978, 15)

And, again, on page one of *Law's Empire*, he observes:

> There is inevitably a moral dimension to an action at law, and so a standing risk of a distinct form of public injustice. A judge must decide not just who shall have what, but who has behaved well, who has met the responsibilities of citizenship, and who by design or greed or insensitivity has ignored his own responsibilities to others or exaggerated theirs to him. If this judgment is unfair, then the community has inflicted a moral injury on one of its members because it has stamped him in some degree or dimension an outlaw. The injury is gravest when an innocent person is convicted of a crime, but it is substantial enough when a plaintiff with a sound claim is turned away from court or a defendant leaves with an undeserved stigma. (Dworkin, 1986, 1–2)[19]

From observations such as these Dworkin abstracts that law is fundamentally coercive, in the way it can affect the lives and well-being of its subjects, by imposing its judgments through the state apparatus of courts and those institutions carrying out their decisions. More controversially, Dworkin draws an inference from this observation that the point of law must be to justify the state's use of coercion (Dworkin, 1986, 190). Otherwise, the use of coercion by

---

[19] See also Raz: "Judges, perhaps more than anyone else, follow the law because they believe they are morally required to do so. There can be no other way in which they can justify imprisoning people, interfering with their property, jobs, family relations, and so on, decisions that are the daily fare of judicial life" (Raz, 2009b, 332); and "Clearly courts' decisions affect both defendants or accused and plaintiffs in substantial ways, and every decision by one person which significantly affects the fortunes of others is, whatever else it may be, a moral decision" (Raz, 1995, 327–28).

courts and legal systems in general would fail to be justified in the impact it has on people's lives.

It is well known that Dworkin adopts a morally evaluative approach to understanding law, where the theorist must engage like the participant (such as a judge) in the task of arriving at propositions of law and legal decisions that can bear the weight of justification for the use of state coercion (Dworkin, 1986, 90). It is also well known that, in Dworkin's view, only his account of law as integrity, which maintains that the truth of propositions of law depends on their success in fitting with and justifying (in a moral sense) the set of legal materials or past political decisions of some legal system, is adequate for the job.[20] In Dworkin's words:

> A full political theory of law, then, includes at least two main parts: it speaks both to the *grounds* of law – circumstances in which particular propositions of law should be taken to be sound or true – and to the *force* of law – the relative power of any true proposition of law to justify coercion in different sorts of exceptional circumstance. (Dworkin, 1986, 110)[21]

It is no doubt true that among the tasks of legal theorists and legal officials an understanding and explanation of how law can be morally justified, given its impact on people's lives, must form a part. But must the source of such moral evaluation be constrained by the conditions of fit and justification, which tie the truth of all propositions of law to past political decisions (i.e., legislation and precedents)? This is doubtful.

Many have criticized Dworkin's view for the results it provides in legal systems where the best account of existing law and the best account of the underlying principles of morality which, in that legal system, are taken to justify existing law are by external standards morally objectionable. Principles of racial inequality, sexual inequality, capitalism, colonialism, and many others often serve as the best rationale of whole areas of law and legal systems, historically and presently. Put more bluntly, the morality sometimes implicit or inherent in law may be far from enlightened morality. And since judges (and theorists) are bound by such morality, it looks as if determining whether law in some time or place really does morally justify the use of coercion (assuming for the moment that that is the point of law) depends not on the exercise of sound moral assessment but, as Joseph Raz once claimed, on a kind of institutionalized moral conservatism (Raz, 1995, 223–24; see also Greenberg, 2014, 1306n29).

---

[20] Dworkin writes, "According to law as integrity, propositions of law are true if they figure in or follow from the principles of justice, fairness, and procedural due process that provide the best constructive interpretation of the community's legal practice" (Dworkin, 1986, 225).

[21] We may also note that on Dworkin's account the answers to both parts of a theory of law – the grounds of law and the force of law – involve moral argument.

I believe this is a sound criticism of Dworkin's view and, to my mind, represents a problem that simply cannot be resolved, given the structure and commitments of his theory. While there is some value in offering an account of how judges ought to go about their business of deciding cases as law-appliers while constrained by institutional pressures of varying degrees depending on their legal systems, an account of the normativity of law that seeks to determine, in general and in particular instances, when application of the law is indeed *morally* justified ought not to be constrained by existing law in locating the relevant source of moral standards. On this score, the natural law views of Aquinas and Finnis, which see the relevant source of morality as external to existing, human law, are superior. (Though, again, I am not here endorsing the particular views of morality that Aquinas and Finnis hold, only their shared view that to understand the moral dimension of the normativity of law (i.e., when law's claims to morally obligate subjects are true or justified) requires moral assessment drawn from sources outside of positive law.)

5.2 Inner Morality of Law

Lon Fuller's view of the connection between law and morality, which rests on his idea of the internal morality of law, also sets out to show, though in a very different way from Dworkin, how the creation and existence of law itself contains the morality it needs to morally bind subjects and deliver morally sound laws. In Fuller's view, there are eight formal or procedural principles all of which all laws must meet, to some degree, to count as laws at all. As Fuller writes, "A total failure in any one of these eight directions does not simply result in a bad system of law; it results in something that is not properly called a legal system at all . . ." (Fuller, 1969, 39). These principles of the internal morality of law are familiar principles of the rule of law and worth briefly rehearsing (Fuller, 1969, ch. 2). Laws must be (i) general; (ii) open or public; (iii) prospective; (iv) clear; (v) free of contradiction; (vi) compliance-possible (i.e., within the powers of subjects to obey); (vii) stable; and (viii) there must be congruence between laws as announced and how they are applied or enforced.

These principles, as Fuller understands them, are essentially the conditions that legislators and judges need to respect for law to fulfil its purpose of "subjecting human conduct to the governance of rules" (Fuller, 1969, 74, 106). When correctly adhered to by legislators and judges, the principles in turn provide nonofficials with moral reasons to obey the law.

Similar to the natural law theories of Aquinas and Finnis, Fuller's theory of law is very much a teleological one and maintains that law must be understood always and everywhere in terms of its moral purpose. And like Aquinas and Finnis, the focus of Fuller's theory is moral evaluation – to show under what conditions subjects have a moral reason to comply with human-made law. But unlike Aquinas and Finnis, Fuller sees the relevant morality not as external to or preexisting actual law but as formally or procedurally tied to its creation and operation. Substantively morally just laws, and in turn the moral obligation to obey law, are generated by careful adherence to the eight principles. In Fuller's view, this is the special way in which law itself creates moral reasons to follow it.

Much as it is with Dworkin's view, something goes quite wrong with supposing that a special morality, internal to law, is the best route to demonstrating and securing the moral value or moral normativity of law as the grounds that create a moral obligation to follow it. Two of Fuller's own examples help to show why. First, he reports from a study about the racial classification laws in South Africa during apartheid that at one time there were approximately 100,000 cases for which no clear or consistent categorization had been made and therefore remained pending (Fuller, 1969, 160). This made it impossible for the racial classification laws to operate. The problem, as Fuller maintains, is that the concept of race is itself insufficiently precise, scientific, or clear; that it renders any law that attempts to discriminate on the basis of race a violation of the principle of clarity, and hence a failure of legality. In this way, and in service of Fuller's aim to show that conformity with formal or procedural moral values can yield conformity with substantive moral values, racist laws are ruled out as illegal and unjust.

Yet surely moral appraisal of law is misguided if approached in the way Fuller proposes. First, legal systems are especially good at drawing clear, even if morally arbitrary, distinctions where clarity in reality might be lacking. This is part of what law is meant to do, and many legal systems have found ways to make clear (at least to themselves) who belongs in what racial category (for example, simply add another factor, such as ancestry or parentage, income, place of residence, and, in the face of insufficient evidence, create default categorizations). But this is not the main problem with Fuller's line of analysis. The more sound and sensible route to showing the wrongness with racially discriminatory laws that disadvantage members of a particular race is not to show that attempts to use them run afoul of the principle of clarity; the wrongness is in the thought and attempt to have them at all, since they represent an affront to equality and human dignity. To see such wrongness requires first-order moral analysis and argument, not pursuit of some special, anemic moral values of law. Think of it this way: even if racially discriminatory laws could be crystal clear – for example, if racial classifications admitted of no indeterminacy or dispute – they would still be obviously morally objectionable as violations of first-order, external moral principles of equality and human dignity.

Fuller provides a second example of how he believes adherence to a formal principle of legality can lead to satisfaction of substantive moral aims. Commenting on the famous Hart–Devlin debate in England in the 1950s over the decriminalization of prostitution and homosexuality, he writes:

> A perennial debate relates to the problem of "legislating morals." Recently there has been a lively discussion of the proper relation of the law to sexual behavior and more particularly to homosexual practices. I must confess that I find this argument quite inconclusive on both sides, resting as it does on initial assumptions that are not made explicit in the argument itself. I would, however, have no difficulty in asserting that the law ought not to make it a crime for consenting adults to engage privately in homosexual acts. The reason for this conclusion would be that any such law simply cannot be enforced and its existence on the books would constitute an open invitation to blackmail, so that there would be a gaping discrepancy between the law as written and its enforcement in practice. I suggest that many related issues can be resolved in similar terms without our having to reach agreement on the substantive moral issues involved. (Fuller, 1969, 132–33)

In this example a substantive moral issue is not so much resolved as evaded entirely, and the debate over the moral value and protections of liberty is simply dismissed in favor of an assessment that any criminalization of sexual practices done in private would invite violation of the congruence principle: that laws on the books must match the laws that are actually practiced and enforced. But this quick account of the issue of sexual freedom gets things wrong. It presumes that a firm value of privacy is already respected regarding private dwellings. This need not be the case in all instances, and can be precarious, especially if societies find the need to violate privacy in the name of other objectives. A first-order moral debate is required here, of precisely the kind Hart and Devlin engaged in. Reliance on a formal principle of legality is too weak but, more importantly, badly misguided as a route to settling questions of moral justification of laws (and the moral reasons they do or do not create for subjects to follow them).

More generally, Fuller argues that adherence to the formal principles of legality will, necessarily, represent a basic level of respect for human dignity. As he explains:

> To embark on the enterprise of subjecting human conduct to the governance of rules involves of necessity a commitment to the view that man is, or can become, a responsible agent, capable of understanding and following rules, and answerable for his defaults ... Every departure from the principles of the

> law's inner morality is an affront to man's dignity as a responsible agent. To
> judge his actions by unpublished or retrospective laws, or to order him to do
> an act that is impossible, is to convey to him your indifference to his powers
> of self-determination. (Fuller, 1969, 162)

It is of course true that trying to govern someone through the use of rules will
require respect for the principles of legality Fuller identifies, which in turn can
be explained as recognition of a subject's capacity for reason as a responsible
agent. But this presumes that the law treats someone as a subject in the first
place, as subject to the rules created and enforced. This is not always the case,
for the law can also treat people not as subjects but as objects (Raz, 2009a, 221).
When people are treated as objects, the rules are about them but not for them.
Treating people as property – for example, as slaves – is a clear example. What
kind of argument would we need to show that slavery laws are an affront to
human dignity and that they ought not to exist (even if they might conform to the
eight principles of the inner morality of law)? Here, it would certainly be
a stretch, and display an alarming lack of moral sense, to seek an argument
showing how slavery laws run afoul of formal principles of legality. A first-
order moral argument about the wrongness of treating people as slaves, through
law or otherwise, is more apt.

5.3 Did We Ever Need Third Theories of Law?

To be clear, I am not suggesting that there is no place or need for the general
kinds of investigations that Dworkin and Fuller pursue, and for two reasons.
Both offer morally evaluative theories of law, which are required for understanding law's moral normativity, as I maintained in Part I, and both explore
some of the distinct values that law answers to, whether in the form of a kind of
role morality for judges (Dworkin) or in the form of formal principles that
legislators should always heed (Fuller). Where both lead us astray, however, is
in supposing that such moral evaluation can be performed squarely, primarily,
or exclusively by attending to law's internal values. This, I contend, mistakenly
asks too much of law – that it can provide sufficient moral value all on its own.

Naturally, this is a very quick way to pronounce judgment on two sustained
and influential theories of law, and much more would need to be said to
substantiate my criticisms. This will not be my aim, not least because the
literature surrounding Dworkin and Fuller is absolutely vast. Instead, I want
to suggest that the motivation to seek third theories of law, which overcome the
impasse or deficiencies of natural law and legal positivist debates, largely
dissipates if we take the approach from Part I, which sees natural law theory
and legal positivism as compatibly pluralist. Both views, as I tried to illustrate,

accept that human positive law (i) has a distinct and important social existence and (ii) is morally fallible. Both views also accept that (iii) the moral standards (whatever their source – God's will, natural principles of reason, the principle of utility, etc.) needed to assess the moral success or failure of human positive law are to be found in sources external to the law itself, since the law's human creation, on its own and no matter how sophisticated our theories of its social existence, is insufficient to give rise to any moral obligations. These three areas of agreement are best understood as commitments to pluralism in the explanation and understanding of the normativity of law. To the extent that Dworkin and Fuller have correctly identified internal values to law, their views must be connected to external standards of morality to offer persuasive accounts of the moral normativity of law.

6 Social Facts and the Normativity of Law

The last twenty-five years in mainstream philosophy of law have seen an increase in work on the problem of the normativity of law, with ever-increasing sophistication. Recent accounts in the positivist tradition, which all accept that law must ultimately be explained in terms of social facts, explore law's character as a special kind of convention, shared cooperative activity, social plan, and institutionalized artifact, all in an attempt to explain the precise way in which law gives its subjects reasons for action. This section will critically survey three such accounts, though it will not be my aim to evaluate the detailed arguments of each view. Instead, I shall question how all frame the problem of the normativity of law – namely, as the problem of explaining the normativity of a social practice, whereby law, as law and nothing else, can be understood to create more than just legal reasons, but bona fide, robust, or even moral reasons as well. Against the background established in Part I, this conception of the problem of the normativity of law is best viewed as a needless invention.

6.1 Shared Cooperative Activities

Part II of Jules Coleman's *The Practice of Principle* stands out as particularly important in the twenty-first-century development of legal positivism for the way he outlines and seeks to defend two key claims:

> All contemporary positivists accept that the criteria of legality are conventional; most also accept what I call the practical difference thesis. Roughly, the practical difference thesis is the claim that law must be able to make a practical difference as law: that is, a difference in the reasons for action that apply to those to whom the law is directed. Taken together, the claim that the criteria of

legality are conventional and the practical difference thesis provide an interpretation of the banal and unobjectionable truth that law is a normative social
practice: Understanding the criteria of law as conventional is a way of inter-
preting the sense in which law is a normative *social* practice; while the practical
difference thesis can similarly be thought of as an interpretation of the sense in
which law is a *normative* social practice. (Coleman, 2001, 68–69)

Coleman defends a version of inclusive legal positivism – the view that conformity with substantive moral values can be among the conventional criteria of
legality in a legal system – which he believes is compatible with these two
claims. The success of his defense is not our concern here. What is of particular
interest is the way in which he frames the problem of explaining the normativity
of the social practice of law. He begins by distinguishing three questions. First,
there is the question of how law, or legal authority, is possible: "The law
purports to govern our conduct, and to do so in virtue of its status as law. The
first question of jurisprudence is: how is that possible?" (Coleman, 2001, 70).
The answer cannot be to appeal to some prior, authorizing rule, for that would
lead to an infinite regress. Better focused, "[t]he first question, then, is how to
explain the *possibility* of legal authority without appealing to legal authority
itself" (Coleman, 2001, 70). The second question of jurisprudence follows from
the first and asks, "*in what way* does law purport to govern conduct? Is there
something distinctive about the kind of authority law claims, and if so, what is
it?" (Coleman, 2001, 71). Coleman rules out the provision of sanctions as an
answer to this question, noting again that the authority to sanction would need to
depend on some prior rule authorizing the use of sanctions. Instead, Coleman
believes the answer must draw upon law's nature as a kind of practical authority: "The distinctive feature of law's governance on this view is that it purports
to govern by *creating reasons for action*" (Coleman, 2001, 71). The third
question asks under what conditions, if any, "the reasons the law purports to
create are moral reasons" (Coleman, 2001, 72). An answer to this last question
would provide an account of the conditions of legitimate authority. It is important to note, however, that the third question receives no further attention and is
effectively omitted from Coleman's account, which addresses only the first two
questions. This move has significant consequences.

It is of course quite helpful to distinguish different questions, for their
confusion can set us back rather than take us forward. But distinction can
sometimes turn into isolation, in a way that ignores, detrimentally, important
relations among the questions and their answers. By focusing on the rule of
recognition, which has become a central theoretical tool among positivists in
explanation of the foundation of legal authority, Coleman proceeds to settle the

precise sense in which a rule of recognition is reason-giving and therefore normative:

> It is a further and important philosophical question how, or in virtue of what feature, a rule purports to be reason-giving. In the case of the rules of critical morality, the claim to provide reasons for action derives from the claim to truth; or, put slightly differently, from the fact that such rules can express bona fide moral reasons independently of whether or not anyone heeds them. The existence of such rules as normative entities does not require that they be practiced or accepted. The opposite is true of social rules, however, whose existence as regulative rules always depends on their being accepted and practiced. This is important in the present context because the rule of recognition is, according to positivists, a social rule and not a rule of critical morality. (Coleman, 2001, 86)

Coleman continues, "The rule of recognition can be a reason for action only if social rules can be reasons for action. What we need is an account of how social rules, which purport to be reasons for action independently of their content, can nevertheless be bona fide reasons" (Coleman, 2001, 86). It is at this point that Coleman argues that to explain the normativity of law – that is, to explain how a social rule such as the rule of recognition creates reasons for action – we need some notion of a conventional social practice in which the very structure of that practice, understood in terms of the beliefs and intentions of its participants, creates reasons for action. Several ideas are introduced to build this explanation. First, there is Margaret Gilbert's idea of two people taking a walk together:

> Part of what distinguishes this activity from the activity of two people who are simply walking alongside one another is that the former activity has a normative structure that the latter lacks. If you and I are taking a walk together, your actions and intentions create reasons for me, and mine create reasons for you. For example, the fact that you turn to the left – or even that you intend or prefer to do so – can give me a reason to turn left. Similarly, when judges adopt the practice of applying the rule of recognition, the actions and intentions of the other judges are reasons for each; it is as though they are going for a walk together, rather than simply walking alongside one another. (Coleman, 2001, 91)

Applying this view, Coleman suggests that the notion of a rule of recognition might be usefully explained as a type of coordination convention:

> In the present context the importance of coordinative conventions is that the actions of some whose behavior is governed by them can be reasons for others. Thus, the fact that the other motorists drive on the right side of the road typically gives me a reason for doing so as well; the fact that everyone else in our group is going to the opera gives me a reason for doing so as well; and so

> on. Coordinative conventions create normative relationships of just the sort
> officials – especially judges – appear to have toward one another. (Coleman,
> 2001, 92)

However, Coleman maintains that the account of the rule of recognition as
a kind of coordination convention, while on the right track, ultimately falls
short, since it is too weak to capture properly the kinds of reasons officials have
in carrying on their practices (Coleman, 2001, 95). To achieve success, he draws
on the yet more elaborate notion, introduced by Michael Bratman, of a shared
cooperative activity. Shared cooperative activities are, as Bratman explains
them, a special kind of social practice, which have three characteristic features
(Bratman, 1992). These are mutual responsiveness, commitment to the joint
activity, and commitment to mutual support. We need not explore the details of
these characteristics, but need only note that they are deeper ways of explaining
how joint intentions, beliefs, and actions constitute normative social practices.

One final piece is needed to complete this brief summary of Coleman's view
of how social practices on their own can generate "bona fide" reasons. He
believes that the internal point of view, a key part of Hart's explanation of social
rules, is sufficient to explain how reasons – and normativity – are generated, but
only once we understand the internal point of view "as the exercise of a basic
and important psychological capacity of human beings to adopt a practice or
pattern of behavior as a norm ... Understood in this more sophisticated
sense ... the internal point of view is essential to the explanation of the rule
of recognition's normativity" (Coleman, 2001, 88–89). To illustrate, Coleman
provides the example of a personal rule to do 100 sit-ups every day:

> By thus adopting my behavior as a norm (and provided I regularly conform
> to it) I have made the behavior a rule or norm for me. In doing so, I have
> created a reason that is additional to and different from the reasons of fitness
> and health that I already had. The internal point of view creates an analogous
> reason for those who adopt it. In this sense, the internal point of view actually
> *does* "turn behavior into a rule"; it turns a social fact into a normative one.
> (Coleman, 2001, 89; footnote omitted)

I will confess, no matter how many times I read this passage, I cannot get from
A to B, from behavior plus belief to some kind of new reason. It is important to
be clear here that these additional reasons are to be understood as real, genuine,
"bona fide" reasons and not just beliefs on the part of the agent that they have
reasons (i.e., "taking myself to have a new reason"). But how exactly, we might
ask, is this possible? How, in other words, is the move to be made from a belief
that I have a reason to do something (and that I do it) to actually having such
a reason? If anything, we seem to have an illicit move from fact to value or from

is to *ought*. Maybe such a move is possible in this context, or maybe not. I will leave that aside, for there is a more important issue to be raised about Coleman's general approach to the problem of the normativity of law. As we saw above, Coleman not only distinguishes between moral reasons and the special kind of social reasons that he believes law creates, but he also isolates these social reasons, in the sense that he does not connect them to moral or other kinds of reasons. It is worth noting that this is a clear departure from Raz's view, introduced in Section 4, in which the reasons created by law are to be understood as second-order reasons, which depend for their existence and normativity on first-order reasons (of which morality is a key kind for law). To use the motorist example, I do have a reason to follow the rule and drive on the right side if others do, as Coleman notes. But, and this is what Coleman misses when he presents the example, this reason is of a second-order kind, and only has the normativity it does because of the underlying, first-order moral reason of avoiding harm (i.e., safety). Any explanation of the rule of driving on the right side of the road that ignores the rule's connection to its underlying reason misunderstands both the role the rule plays in practical reason (by specifying how to avoid harm) and the rule's normativity (as resting on the underlying reason of avoiding harm). Coleman's narrow focus on social practice alone obscures this crucial point.

6.2 The Planning Theory

A decade later Scott Shapiro identifies a similar kind of challenge to legal positivism, or any theory that attempts to explain the normativity of law using a social fact theory, though he is much more aware of the problem I have just identified with Coleman's view:

> According to the legal positivist, the content of the law is ultimately determined by social facts alone. To know the law, therefore, one must (at least in principle) be able to derive this information exclusively from knowledge of social facts. But knowledge of the law is normative whereas knowledge of social facts is descriptive. How can normative knowledge be derived exclusively from descriptive knowledge? That would be to derive judgments about what one legally *ought* to do from judgments about what socially *is* the case. Legal positivism, therefore, appears to violate the famous principle introduced by David Hume (often called "Hume's Law"), which states that one can never derive an ought from an is. (Shapiro, 2011, 47)

Shapiro describes this issue as "an extremely serious challenge to legal positivism," and one which many prominent positivist theories fail to overcome. For example, after lengthy analysis, Shapiro concludes that Hart's attempt to describe law as a normative social practice collapses:

> We can see that Hart's attempt to distinguish the legal from the moral is seriously flawed. For once we focus on the role that legal judgments and claims play in social life, it becomes hard to deny that they are constituted not only by normative concepts and terms, but by moral ones as well. Ironically, then, Hart's solution to Hume's Challenge actually undermines the positivistic project. For if legal judgments are normative judgments, they must be moral judgments as well. And if they are moral judgments, then the critique of the law whose very possibility positivists hoped to secure would forever be beyond their reach. (Shapiro, 2011, 115)

If sound, this is of course just about as damning a criticism of Hart's view as one can imagine – that he cannot maintain a prized positivistic distinction between legal judgments and moral judgments. But something has gone wrong here, in a similar way to what went wrong with Coleman's view. I do not intend to work through Shapiro's arguments, but simply question his starting point, as I did with Coleman. In presenting Hart's view, Shapiro writes, "How can normative judgments about legal rights and obligations be derived from purely descriptive judgments about social practices? . . . Curiously, as central as this question is to the success of Hart's jurisprudential project, he does not openly address it. In all of his many writings, he never explicitly explains how his positivistic theory is compatible with Hume's Law" (Shapiro, 2011, 97). But instead of supposing that Hart overlooked a central problem, another way to understand things would be to suppose that Hart recognized there was no problem to begin with. While I have enormous respect for the many contributions both Coleman and Shapiro have made to general jurisprudence, on the particular issue of how they frame the problem of the normativity of law I believe they have simply fabricated a problem that does not exist. To Shapiro's question, "How can normative knowledge be derived exclusively from descriptive knowledge?" the answer is that there is no derivation, or inference, that was ever envisioned by Hart because no derivation was ever needed. Description of the law is just description, "even when what is described is an evaluation" (Hart, 2012, 244). More forcefully, in explaining the legal positivist proposition (LP*) that the validity of any norm in a legal system depends on its sources, not its merits, John Gardner writes:

> Proposition (LP*), although a proposition about the conditions of validity of certain norms that may be used in practical reasoning, is itself normatively inert. It does not provide any guidance at all on what anyone should do about anything on any occasion . . . I don't just mean that it provides no moral guidance. It provides no legal guidance either . . . Lawyers and law teachers find this comprehensive normative inertness in (LP*) hard to swallow. (Gardner, 2012, 24)

Not just lawyers and law teachers but, unfortunately, some legal theorists as well. The problem of the normativity of law has many dimensions, but trying to construct a derivation or draw an inference from a descriptive explanation of law to what ought to be done, as a matter of practical reason (legal, moral, prudential, etc.), *from that descriptive explanation alone* is simply not one of them.

Again, I suspect that the urge to explain law's normativity in a way that generates real, "bona fide" reasons while remaining within a positivist framework is no doubt an attempt to say more about law's normativity without slipping into a natural law framework. But as I suggested in Part I, legal positivism and natural law theory are in agreement here, so such a project loses its motivation. Neither, as we saw, attempts to derive any reasons about what ought to be done, in response to the claims of human, positive law, on the basis of human, positive law alone. This will not change, no matter the degree of sophistication in the explanation of human, positive law. External moral standards are required, whatever their source might be. Consider again the example of motorists all driving on the right side of the road. As Coleman says, motorists have a reason to drive on the right side of the road given that others are doing so. True, but to repeat one last time, the rule that we ought to drive on the right side of the road is only a second-order reason, dependent on a first-order moral reason of safety (in Raz's terms), or a human, positive law whose force depends on conformity with a natural law of avoiding harm (in Aquinas's or Finnis's terms). In the absence of a first-order reason or natural law such as safety or avoidance of harm, the mere fact that others are behaving in a certain way gives rise to no reason (of any kind) to behave so as well.

This is a crucial claim of this Element: that some recent positivist accounts of the problem of the normativity of law have led us astray. One last example should suffice.[22] In *The Functions of Law*, Ken Ehrenberg offers a state-of-the-art theory of law's functions, which identifies and corrects the mistakes of much previous work on whether law can be profitably understood through a functionalist lens. His book sets the bar for any future analysis of law's functionality. At one point, however, Ehrenberg adopts a conception of the problem of the normativity of law similar to that of Coleman and Shapiro, though, unlike them, Ehrenberg finds the answer in law's nature as an "institutionalized abstract artifact." Seeing law in this way, as a special formation of authors' and participants' beliefs and intentions, is precisely what we need, Ehrenberg maintains, to explain law's ability to "create new reasons for action" for its subjects (Ehrenberg, 2016, 8). These new reasons

---

[22] The discussion in the next few paragraphs is drawn from Giudice, 2019. I would like to thank Oxford University Press for permission to reuse part of this review.

typically come in the form of new rights and duties, yet they are not to be understood simply as context-restricted legal reasons, where one simply claims that, "according to the law, you have a reason to X, but outside the law, there may or may not be any reason to X." Instead, Ehrenberg aims to explain how legal reasons can generate "robust obligations" or "robust normativity" (Ehrenberg, 2016, 3), and in that way can "break through" their contextual bounds:

> But our question . . . is whether and how a particular legal reason might break through to be a newly created objective normative reason for anyone to whom the law is addressed. To say that it is an objective reason for those to whom it is addressed is to imply that it has a moral character of trumping at least some other reasons held by them. (Ehrenberg, 2016, 152)

Of course, not all legal reasons will succeed in "breaking though"; law is fallible in this way, as Ehrenberg notes. But is it true that in other instances law does or can succeed, so creating "wholly," "truly," or "entirely" new reasons, even some with a "moral character" (Ehrenberg, 2016, 152, 154, 179)? Here, I think there is reason to doubt. Take this example offered by Ehrenberg:

> If I already have a reason to provide for my family and the law tells me that the way to do this is to make a will and that for my will to be recognized by the law it must be signed by two witnesses, I now have a reason I didn't have before to make a will and have it signed by two witnesses. (Ehrenberg, 2016, 154)

The law about wills certainly adds something here, but there is another way to describe the addition: the law did not create any new reasons but simply gave me a *new course of action* that would help me comply with my original reason – to provide for my family. I do not think anything turns on resolving these competing descriptions, and actually prefer as well to describe the law as a reason for action. But it is misleading to call the law a "wholly," "truly," or "entirely" new reason, since the law would not count as a reason at all (in the "robust," "break through" sense) absent the original reason to provide for one's family (see also Enoch, 2011).

The thought that law could create entirely new reasons, *of a robust, objective normative kind*, as Ehrenberg supposes is possible, diverges from how positivists such as Hart and Raz understood the problem of explaining legal normativity. For them, it is not a problem of explaining how law on its own can create new robust reasons (moral or otherwise). Of course, neither Hart nor Raz denies that legal philosophers ought to develop an understanding of when (if ever) there are objective reasons to obey the law, but both deny that the answer will ever be found in an account of law's existence as such. An objective reason to obey the law requires an objective premise in one's practical reasoning, and the social fact of law on its own is no such premise.

Ehrenberg rejects this conception of the problem of explaining legal normativity as unsatisfying, as it does "not sit well with the way we understand law as a possibly sometimes legitimate practical authority" (Ehrenberg, 2016, 3). Instead, he opts for a more controversial understanding of the objective of legal positivism: we need to understand how to derive "normative conclusions" from "merely descriptive premises" (Ehrenberg, 2016, 4) and, more generally, that "[w]hile other areas of philosophy tend to work firmly on one or the other side of the gap, legal philosophy must contend with how to get from facts to norms" (Ehrenberg, 2016, 4). Again, I am afraid I am just not convinced. It is true that we need explanations of *both* law as fact *and* law as norm. But it is not true that we need to explain how to get *from* law as fact *to* law as norm. As we saw in Part I, both prominent natural law theorists and legal positivists agree that to explain law's moral normativity requires moral premises and not just identification of what has been posited or created as a matter of social fact, however the notion of a social fact is to be understood. By ignoring the history, Ehrenberg, like Coleman and Shapiro, has invented (or perhaps simply adopted) a problem that does not and need not exist.

There is another argument to be made in favor of sticking with the views of Aquinas, Finnis, Hart, and Raz on the moral normativity of law, and it is similar to the criticism I offered against the views of Dworkin and Fuller. There, I argued that the moral normativity they tried to generate from within the practice of law itself, whether in terms of its content (Dworkin) or its form (Fuller), severely weakened, and generally did a disservice to, the importance of moral justification and criticism of law. Law is certainly morally significant, in the way that it can impact and affect people's lives, interests, and well-being. To try to generate robust normativity through social facts alone, whether understood as shared cooperative activities, plans, or institutionalized abstract artifacts, is simply too weak a basis, and for that reason is misguided. Law must be respected, theoretically and practically, for the nature it has, and therefore requires an appropriate approach and method for its study and explanation. Law is not like taking a walk or cooking together; it is much more morally important than that.

Within the confines of this short section, it is not possible to trace all the arguments and lines of analysis in the views of Coleman, Shapiro, and Ehrenberg, and, as such, what I say here might be taken as mere fighting words. If so, so be it. But I do hope to have provided enough of a case that by viewing some of the overlap between prominent natural law theorists (Aquinas and Finnis) and legal positivists (Hart and Raz) we can appreciate how recent positivist accounts have invented a pseudo problem of the normativity of law – namely, by trying to derive normativity (moral, extralegal, etc.) from law's existence alone. What makes this conclusion particularly interesting is that it is the same mistake, though coming from a different direction, as we saw in Section 5. Both Dworkin and Fuller also attempted to derive normativity (for them, squarely of the moral kind) from law's existence. Of course, the arguments of Aquinas, Finnis, Hart, and Raz are in need of much elaboration and development, but at least they were correct (and agreed) on this score: the reasons generated by social practices such as law are second-order reasons, which depend for their robust normativity on the existence and conformity with first-order reasons, primarily those of morality (but often reasons of prudence as well). I submit that this part of the philosophy of law does not need fixing.

7 Coercion and Law's Normativity

Part II of this Element is devoted to identification of what I take to be some misguided steps in the direction of work on the normativity of law, and this section is no exception, though the kind of misguided step I wish to explain is of a different kind. It concerns the focused energies on nailing down whether coercion must figure centrally (read essentially, necessarily) in a theory about the nature or concept of law. I want to suggest that while this debate has some value, it has, mainly for methodological reasons, obscured from view an important way in which debates about the normativity of law can and must be broadened.

7.1 Coercion and the Concept of Law

Part of the history of the debate over the role of coercion in legal theory is quite familiar. In the classical legal positivist theories of Jeremy Bentham and John Austin, the notions of imperatives or commands figured prominently as key to understanding the nature of law. Both Bentham and Austin maintained that directives accompanied by threats of force in the event of noncompliance were the essential mode of existence and operation of law and were always traceable back to some sovereign who stood outside any chain of coercion. Command or imperative theories of law remained dominant in the English-speaking world for well over a century, until H. L. A. Hart's thorough and sustained criticism,[23] most fully developed in *The Concept of Law*, altered the course of legal positivism.

---

[23] Though as Fred Schauer notes, Hart's criticisms of Bentham and Austin were not entirely novel, as many had been raised well before *The Concept of Law* (Schauer, 2015, 23–26).

Hart's criticisms of Austin's command theory of law identified several defects, which are important to rehearse briefly for they reveal an important theme. The first defect can be found by considering the typical range of application of laws, which shows that even lawmakers are often subject to the laws they create. For example, it might be thought that criminal laws – laws specifying which serious acts of violence or harm are prohibited under threat of punishment – provide a good example of how the command theory of law works, since they seem to be instances of orders backed up by the threat of a negative sanction. But, as Hart explains, most criminal statutes do not resemble a set of orders backed by threats, since criminal laws also typically apply to those who have created them. It does not make sense, Hart added, to say that lawmakers are threatening themselves.

A second defect emerges from observation of the variety of laws typically found in a legal system. Hart notes that not all laws prescribe or prohibit behavior under threat of sanction. Some laws, for example, such as rules providing for the making of contracts, marriages, and wills, do not demand a certain behavior but serve to facilitate certain transactions. These "power-conferring" rules are fundamentally misunderstood if explained as orders backed by threats. As Hart says, power-conferring rules do not say "Do this whether you wish to or not," but rather "If you wish to do this, this is the way to do it" (Hart, 2012, 28).

A third defect concerns the mode of origin of laws and challenges the idea that all laws originate from a sovereign. Some legal rules (e.g., customary laws) develop in ways that are not connected to the top-down acts of an uncommanded commander. Merchants' rules of commerce, for example, have often arisen out of the needs and practices of the merchants themselves.

A fourth defect is visible with the core notion of a sovereign. Identifying such a person or group of persons is a misguided pursuit in many societies. For example, in modern liberal democracies it is not possible to identify the sovereign with either the legislature (which is bound by its own rules) or the electorate (because it does not make sense to say that the electorate commands and obeys itself). While there are of course hierarchical relationships in modern legal systems, sovereignty, as Austin understood, is often illusory.

In one way or another, there is a common thread running through these criticisms, and it is that in Austin's theory there is the assumption that law is always imposed and never accepted. Hart's well-known account of the internal point of view and social rules took as its starting point this fundamental defect.

Hart's criticisms of Austin's view stood for a long time as conclusive, though recently some have pushed back in an attempt to show that there is indeed a conceptual, necessary connection between law and coercion, or at least a connection much stronger than Hart recognized. Kenneth Himma, for example, acknowledges that it might be possible to imagine a society of angels that exists and functions without any kind of coercive backing whatsoever. But ours is not a society of angels, Himma points out (Himma, 2020, ch. 10). Conceptual analysis of law, the predominant method of analytical legal theorists, is an exercise in understanding "our" concept of law, the concept we use to make sense of our practices that create law, and such analysis reveals that coercion is in fact a necessary feature of law. Ekow Yankah similarly argues that "coercive sanctions are a necessary and perhaps the most important feature for explaining legal norms" (Yankah, 2008, 1197). And while rejecting a tight conceptual connection, Kara Woodbury-Smith maintains that law is nonetheless necessarily "coercion-apt" (Woodbury-Smith, 2020).[24]

Others accept the observation that law and coercion do not stand in a strictly necessary or conceptual relation, but maintain instead that a sound theory about the nature or concept of law must take as its commitment explanation of important features of law, which may or may not be necessary. Such an account is powerfully presented by Frederick Schauer, who highlights that while coercion might not be a strictly necessary feature of law wherever and whenever it exists, it is certainly an important and pervasive feature, which has several implications for our understanding and moral evaluation of law. Schauer acknowledges that this makes the question of law's relation to coercion largely, or at least equally, of an empirical nature, but no less significant a part of legal theory for that reason.

7.2 Normative v. Predictive: A False Dichotomy?

I do not want to denigrate the conceptual debate about law's relation to coercion. It is well worth pursuing the question about whether particular laws, especially those requiring or prohibiting certain forms of conduct, must be backed up by sanctions to qualify as laws at all, or whether, at the level of legal systems, some kind of coercion (perhaps in the form of centralization over the rightful use of force) must be present. These are important questions demanding conceptual investigation.[25] It is also well worth reflecting on whether some third category of claim, neither purely conceptual nor purely empirical, must be advanced about law's relation to coercion, such as Hart thought when he introduced the idea of natural (as opposed to conceptual or metaphysical) necessity (Hart, 2012, 199).

---

[24] See also Gkouvas, 2023. Gkouvas argues that before questions about the necessity or contingency of the relation between law and coercion can be answered, we must first address disagreements about the methods and aims of particular theories of law.

[25] The leading account is Himma, 2020.

I want to suggest, however, that the conceptual debate may have reached its limits, at least from the perspective of our topic, which is the normativity of law. This is not a bad thing either. For whether it is only some legal norms that must be backed up by coercion to be laws, or whether it is only some legal systems that must have centralized enforcement mechanisms, such identification is sufficient to frame empirical questions about the role that coercion plays in motivating actors to comply with those laws or take seriously those legal systems. There is also the more general question about the conditions under which coercion is most likely to be needed to secure compliance with law, or under what conditions coercion might compromise law's efforts to secure genuinely peaceful coexistence or voluntary acceptance of law (or acceptance of law for the right reasons, we might say). And there is also, as noted in Section 2, the prudentially evaluative question of asking when it is in our self-interest to comply with law or not.

To put such questions squarely into the mix in an investigation into the normativity of law requires some work, and in particular a return to Hart's critique of Austin to identify aspects that tend not to figure in the conceptual debate about whether coercion is a necessary feature of law. In addition to the criticisms that Austin's command theory failed to explain the scope of application, variety, origins, and typical sources of law, Hart also argued that Austin's theory was flawed in approach and method. Hart maintained that a focus on sanctions – a cornerstone of the command theory – was to adopt an external point of view. In his famous illustration, Hart contrasts the external point of view with the internal point of view as follows:

> What the external point of view, which limits itself to the observable regularities of behavior, cannot reproduce is the way in which the rules function as rules in the lives of those who normally are the majority of society. These are the officials, lawyers, or private persons who use them, in one situation after another, as guides to the conduct of social life, as the basis for claims, demands, admissions, criticism, or punishment, viz., in all the familiar transactions of life according to rules. For them the violation of a rule is not merely a basis for the prediction that a hostile reaction will follow but a *reason* for hostility. (Hart, 2012, 90)

Identification of the internal aspect of rules has been taken by many as a major advancement in legal theory (Dickson, 2001, 24) and a decisive objection to Austin's sanction-based account of legal obligation. It has also been taken to be key to identifying and isolating the problem of the normativity law, to explain exactly how law, on its own and independently of sanctions, gives rise to reasons for action, as Hart envisions in the passage above.

For our purposes, we can notice two beliefs, or commitments, that have followed from Hart's criticism of Austin. First, an explanation of law that focuses on sanctions is an explanation of law from the external point of view and, as such, cannot account for the normative dimension of law as a form of rational, reason-based guidance. Whatever else they are – perhaps a form of psychological factor – sanctions are not reasons. Second, and relatedly, a predictive theory of law, which Hart supposes is the kind of theory of legal obligation Austin offers, according to which to be under a legal obligation means that a subject is likely to suffer negative consequences for noncompliance, has nothing to do with explaining the normativity of law. Hart's argument against a predictive theory of legal obligation is of course familiar: as he correctly pointed out, it made perfect sense to think that someone was still under a legal obligation even though they stood no chance of being caught or punished in breaking the law.

I believe Hart is right to note the ways in which some dimensions of the normativity of law require an approach from the internal point of view – namely, to explain the circumstances where law is accepted and not experienced as imposed through the use of negative sanctions or coercion. But I believe he is mistaken to suppose that the external point of view, and a focus on negative sanctions, is necessarily about something other than the normativity of law. For, as I have been stressing throughout this Element, the problem of the normativity of law is many, not one. One of the problems, or dimensions, is investigation into the presence and role of sanctions as themselves reasons for action (of a primarily prudential kind). This argument rests on the simple observation that there is nothing amiss in understanding the desire or interest in avoiding a negative sanction threatened by law as itself a reason – even a robust reason – for action (Kramer, 2004, 156, 216–22; Himma, 2020). In turn, if Schauer and others are right to think, as I believe they are, that coercion is one of law's important features (even if not conceptually necessary), then we would do well to see law's coercive means as directly relevant to thinking about how law purports to bind us as rational agents.

Hart's mistake here has been repeated by others. We find Ronald Dworkin, for example, expressing the view in this way:

> We make an important distinction between law and even the general orders of a gangster. We feel that the law's strictures – and its sanctions – are different in that they are obligatory in a way that the outlaw's commands are not. Austin's analysis has no place for any such distinction, because it defines an obligation as subjection to the threat of force, and so founds the authority of law entirely on the sovereign's ability and will to harm those who disobey . . . [But a] *rule differs from an order, among other ways by being normative,* by

setting a standard of behavior that has a call on its subject beyond the threat that may enforce it. A rule can never be binding just because some person with physical power wants it to be so. (Dworkin, 1978, 19–20; emphasis added)

Dworkin of course has a special sense of binding in mind – a moralized notion of binding, as we saw in Section 5 – but once we see normativity in a broader way as including reasons of all kinds, it is hard to deny that threats of negative sanctions also serve as reasons for action. Law is different from the use of mere force in just this way: the gangster could just beat victims and take their money; but if they issue an order, or reply to any questions with "or else I will beat or kill you," they have added an element of normativity to the social situation by appealing to reasons for action.

In some places Hart does offer a more balanced view, or at least indicates that a balanced view would be more sound. For example, he writes:

One of the difficulties facing any legal theory anxious to do justice to the complexity of the facts is to remember the presence of both these points of view and not to define one of them out of existence. Perhaps all our criticisms of the predictive theory of obligation may be best summarized as the accusation that this is what it does to the internal aspect of obligatory rules. (Hart, 2012, 91)

The internal aspect of rules is just one aspect, though a very important aspect, of the normativity of law; but, likewise, the motivation created by sanctions, which can ground predictive (or psychological) accounts of law, is also just one aspect, though a very important aspect (following Schauer), of the normativity of law.

I also want to suggest more generally that while predictive, sanction-based accounts are different, they are not changing the subject from the normativity of law to something else. As a conceptual matter, a sanction can be a reason for action, so any complete theory of the normativity of law would have to accommodate this fact and not risk its outright exclusion. The way Hart draws the distinction between the internal and external points of view, as we saw above, does just this. His distinction sees the internal point of view as uniquely concerned with law as reason, and the external point of view as concerned simply with predictions and therefore not with reasons at all. This is mistaken.

Still, the difference is important to acknowledge. While the avoidance of negative sanctions can be a reason for action, as both a conceptual matter and an evaluative matter, a central interest in coercion in legal theory is also squarely connected to the empirical question of how law affects human behavior in a causal sense. Schauer explains:

After all, law has value as a distinct phenomenon, a distinct institution, and a distinct category largely insofar as it affects human behavior. Perhaps law might be of interest even were it causally inert, because examining a society's laws might reveal some feature of interest of which law was the consequence. From that perspective we might (and perhaps should) be interested in law as indicator and not as cause. Realistically, however, and certainly in this book, our principal interest in law and legal systems lies in their capacity to shape and influence what people do. (Schauer, 2015, 45)

The "causal role of law in influencing behavior" (Schauer, 2015, 57) is a core theme in Schauer's *The Force of Law*, though his conclusion is that law *qua* law, understood in a sanction-independent sense, actually plays very little of a causal role. Negative sanctions or coercion, as he maintains on empirical grounds, actually play a much more decisive role than law itself in getting people to do things they would otherwise not do.

As I have remarked before (Giudice, 2020, 125–26), an interest in explaining the causal role of law and sanctions in influencing people's behavior could see law *qua* law and sanctions as independent and perhaps competing causal forces, as Schauer does. But there is an alternative. The interest might be in seeing how both law *qua* law and sanctions are complementary causal factors in explaining people's obedience, at least when they do obey. This latter approach seems to be a better route, since often the combination of both the causal force of law and the causal force of sanctions is necessary on many occasions. For example, I might be successfully scared by the threat of paying a fine or going to prison if I do not pay my taxes annually, but that fear alone will not get me to obedience, since I will still need to know exactly how much, when, and to whom I ought to make a payment if I am owing in taxes at the end of a calendar year. The particular tax laws, understood as particular rules in a sanction-independent sense, must also play a causal role, alongside the fear of negative sanction, in explaining why I pay my taxes when and how I do. This may not always be the case, of course. For example, some might avoid murder, not because they view it as immoral, but simply because they fear the punishment of going to prison, without knowing the specific rules or definition of the criminal offence of murder or details about the range of sentences, mitigating factors, etc. In such an instance we would have successful deterrence without specific knowledge of the law (beyond knowledge that the law frowns upon killing others). But when the causal factors of law *qua* law and sanctions do combine, as they do in the tax law example, the causal factors are not competitive but complementary, in a way which could be described as a combination of first-order and second-order reasons. If I have a first-order reason to avoid going to prison, then I have a second-order reason to follow the tax laws.

One might persist in objecting, however, that empirical (including predictive) investigations have nothing to do with the normativity of law, as these lie entirely outside the realm of the conceptual and philosophical. We find Jules Coleman, for example, patrolling the boundaries in this way: "Jurisprudence is the study, in part, of how law purports to govern conduct. It is not the study of how law secures individual compliance with the rights and duties it creates by its directives" (Coleman, 2001, 72). This objection fails, but its failure is an instructive one. We might push back and dispute the boundary between what is and what is not part of jurisprudence or the philosophy of law, but I believe a better response is to claim that only some, but not all, questions about the normativity of law fall within jurisprudence or the philosophy of law. Questions about the normativity of law, in other words, are not within the exclusive purview of the philosophy of law. To declare that there could be no empirical, nonphilosophical studies of the normativity of law, simply by fiat, is analytical jurisprudence at its worst. In Section 8 I will attempt to set out a wholistic division of labor more systematically.

PART III
8 Observations and Lessons

As I mentioned in the Introduction, my aim in this Element is not to cut through the diverse conceptions and theories of the problem of the normativity of law in search of the one, true conception and theory. There is simply too much difference across perspectives and methods to pursue such a goal, especially since, as I believe, such differences do not always indicate that some must be making mistakes in need of correction. Instead, such differences ought to be surveyed and, where appropriately responding to multiple dimensions of the normativity of law, respected. Often, such differences mark genuinely important and varied lines of investigation emerging from the nature and character of law itself. To keep this diversity of purpose and method firmly in view, this section will propose a methodological framework for mapping the various kinds of investigations into the normativity of law, drawing on examples from previous sections and adding new ones along the way.

8.1 Imperialism, Difference, and Continuity

The approaches to the problem of the normativity of law surveyed and critically assessed in the preceding sections represent not just different answers to the problem but often different methodological commitments altogether. To the extent that the problem of the normativity of law has several dimensions, a pluralist approach to its study and understanding seems a matter of course.

Though most try to find *the* correct angle from which to explain the normativity of law, some have recognized that we are unlikely to find a one-size-fits-all conception and answer to the problem. For example, Brian Bix writes:

> It may well be that law's double nature – as a social institution and as a reason-giving practice – makes it impossible to capture the nature of law fully through any one approach, with a more "neutral" approach (like legal positivism) required to understand its institutional side, and a more evaluative approach (like natural law theory) required to understand its reason-giving side. (Bix, 2005, 45)

More recently Julie Dickson notes these different questions about the normativity of law:

> (1) questions concerning the meaning of normative statements or of normative language [in law] . . . (2) questions concerning the character of the claims that law makes . . . (3) questions concerning whether and under what conditions law truly is morally binding and truly does provide moral reasons for action of a certain kind, and whether and to what extent it successfully achieves certain moral aims and realizes certain moral values. (Dickson, 2022, 86)

And with some overlap and some divergence, in an article devoted to showing there is no single "problem of the normativity of law," Leslie Green identifies these four questions:

Q1 How could law be normative?
Q2 Which laws are norms?
Q3 What are the relations between legal norms and other norms?
Q4 What could ground a moral obligation to obey legal norms? (Green, 2023)

These are important starts, and offer support to the idea that a pluralist approach is best for understanding the normativity of law in all its dimensions. What I shall do now is examine three general ways of addressing such pluralism. As I will explain, the first two are defective and should be discarded, while the third is most promising.

Imperialism. The views sketched in the preceding sections displayed a range of methodological approaches and commitments in addition to the substantive claims they put forward about the normativity of law. Natural law views, as we saw, adopt morally evaluative perspectives by offering resources to show when law's claims on our obedience are morally justified or not. Legal positivist views, alternatively, adopt descriptive–explanatory and morally neutral perspectives to identify, in a conceptual fashion, the distinctive features and structures of law's claims on our practical reasoning. Antipositivist views, such as those of Dworkin and Fuller, also adopt morally evaluative approaches, but in ways constrained by the substance or formal structure of existing law. Recent positivist views surveyed in Section 6 also try to offer morally neutral conceptual explanations, but in a way that tries to build "genuine," "robust," "bona fide," or "objective" normativity out of social facts. And finally, in Section 7 we encountered an approach, usefully displayed in Schauer's work, which is neither morally evaluative nor primarily conceptual, but empirical instead. As I tried to suggest, not all of these approaches rest on a sound basis. But I do believe that, in general, evaluative, conceptual (in the descriptive–explanatory sense), and empirical approaches are all individually necessary and (perhaps, though I will not argue it here) jointly sufficient for a complete understanding of law's normativity.

There is a discernible tendency in legal theory, however, that attempts to deny such plurality and settle instead on the single, correct method for doing legal theory. This is what Hart aptly termed "imperialism" (Hart, 2012, 243). Imperialism is the attempt to demonstrate the truth of a single approach or method for understanding the nature of law, such that all competing approaches are held to be misguided since they will only distort or misunderstand law's nature. It is also the methodological commitment of trying to reinterpret all competing types of theories as theories of the type deemed to be correct. In earlier work I singled out Dworkin's theoretical commitments as a prime example of imperialism, since at each turn he appears to exclude perfectly viable, though different, approaches to his own (Giudice, 2016). I want to emphasize, however, that imperialistic leanings can be found across all approaches in legal theory, from evaluative to descriptive–explanatory to empirical. In the present context, we can find imperialistic approaches to the normativity of law in attempts to collapse all conceptions of the problem of the normativity of law into one, to nail down a single, univocal problem, *the* normativity of law problem. A recent example provides a useful illustration. In the "Preface" to *The Long Arc of Legality*, David Dyzenhaus takes as his point of departure this central problem he believes a theory of law (and legal positivism in particular) must answer:

> Hobbes, Kelsen and Hart all thought that a theory of law must account for law's authority, but without making such authority depend on a source outside legal order, whether divine will or some secular ideal of justice. Thus, legal positivists traditionally reject rival "natural law" theories because such theories do, in their view, trace the authority of law to some moral source outside legal order. That leaves positivists with the arduous task of solving the puzzle of legal authority – how law transforms might into right – without reliance on anything external to law. (Dyzenhaus, 2022, ix)

The analysis that follows is rich and informative, but Dyzenhaus nowhere pauses to reflect on whether theorists as different as Hobbes, Kelsen, and Hart – all so-called legal positivists – really do see the problem of law's authority (or normativity) in the same way, so needing an answer of the same kind.[26] Taking Hart as just one example, to think that he sees the problem of law's authority as the problem of showing "how law transforms might into right" – a formulation Hart never used and surely would reject – is misguided from the outset. Hart rejected command theories of law, so the idea that law operates everywhere and always as a matter of "might" was not his starting point, but, further, trying to draw inferences from the existence of law to any kind of right flies directly in the face of his positivist insistence that the existence of law gives no answer, on its own, about what anyone (legal official or citizen) ought or has the right to do. Explaining the character of law's existence and claims is one thing; explaining whether it actually gives anyone reasons (especially reasons of justice or morality) to do anything is another. All of this is to say that perhaps we ought to understand Hart (and others) as adopting a different approach to understanding law, and one which is not necessarily in competition with all others. To ignore this and continue with such imperialist twisting of others' views will not advance legal theory but only set it back.

Difference. A second metatheoretical commitment improves upon imperialism but runs into its own problems. It is what we could call, for lack of a better term, the difference view of diversity, which combines (i) the observation that there are many different approaches, methods, and perspectives to understanding law with (ii) the commitment that there is no way to choose between these, since, quite simply, they reflect different aims, methods, and purposes. The difference view we might then describe as a kind of radical relativism or pluralism.

Given the arguments in Sections 5 and 6, it is clearly not a difference view that I endorse, as I believe there are some approaches and methods, such as those of Dworkin, Fuller, Coleman, Shapiro, and Ehrenberg, among others, that are wrongheaded. At the risk of disappointment, I will not attempt to set out any general or particular standards about how to sort acceptable from unacceptable methods or approaches. I only wish to point out that it is not an "anything goes" view that I am proposing; each particular approach and method must in the end be defended, and room for critically appraising each must always be preserved.

Continuity. The view I do endorse is one which appreciates pluralism while remaining critical, yet also seeks to find points of intersection or complementarity between different types of approaches or methods rather than forcing a choice between these. It is a view that values, for example, conceptual explanations of law that at the same time support or frame empirical investigations – which are, in

---

[26] We can also set to one side the question of whether Hobbes, who identifies nineteen laws of nature, actually rejects natural law theory.

other words, very mindful of where empirical study is required to provide evidence or display variation in the phenomena. Similarly, it is a view that values empirically supported conceptual explanations that can inform moral or prudential evaluations of law by identifying precisely where the practice of law is morally fallible or threatening and so full understanding requires moral and prudential assessment. This is all quite abstract, so perhaps an illustration, which continues the discussion from Section 7, will help.

I think Schauer is right to urge us to let go of the obsession with conceptually necessary features of law, particularly in thinking about law and coercion, and turn the question over, at a certain point, to empirical study. But I think there is a way of thinking about conceptual explanation of law that makes this continuity much more vivid and wards off the popular view that conceptual and empirical investigations are simply different projects representing different interests. This is the idea that conceptual explanations of law – indeed, concepts of law – need not be restricted to the search and explanation of conceptually necessary features of law, or conceptually necessary relations, but can also be constructed with contingent features and relations. It is of course true that to talk of a conceptual dimension is to talk about something universal (Russell, 1990, 52), about what is the case everywhere and always, but such a commitment is respected by including, for example, the contingent relation between law and morality: that while law need not satisfy any demands of morality to exist as law in some time or place, it is important everywhere and always to see law as morally fallible or justice apt, given the kind of thing that law is (Green, 2008). Concepts of law are meant to help us understand what law is, to understand what it is to live under and with law, and therefore must draw our attention to their significant and important features and relations, whether these are necessary and essential or contingent but still significant. There is therefore no mistake in supposing that law's contingent relation with morality (and the accompanying understanding of what this means) can and does form part of a universal, conceptual understanding of law.

A similar account can be offered about the relation between law and coercion. It may well be true that there can be laws that exist fully as laws, have the character of law, etc., without being backed up by sanctions (whether centrally or otherwise), or even that there could be entire legal systems, with angel-like subjects, without coercion altogether (again, I do not want to dive into this debate). But even so, it will remain an open question, everywhere and always, whether coercion, where it is present, succeeds in securing compliance with law's requirements, or whether coercion, where it is absent, might need to be introduced to assist with motivating subjects (or officials) to comply with rules, norms, and directives.

It might be objected that contingent relations cannot be included in concepts of law, since a concept of law is meant to demarcate the necessary and essential boundaries of law. All that can be included in a concept of law, in other words, are necessary and essential features. I will confess I find this argument unconvincing, though I think more can be said. First, it is beyond dispute that Hart, in *The Concept of Law*, was attempting to offer an explanation of the concept of law, but of a kind that centered around three "persistent," "recurrent" questions: "How does law differ from and how is it related to orders backed by threats? How does legal obligation differ from, and how is it related to, moral obligation? What are rules and to what extent is law an affair of rules?" (Hart, 2012, 13). To the questions about law's relation to morality and coercion, Hart's answers are that the relations are contingent: laws can exist and function without satisfying demands of morality and without being backed up, everywhere and always, by the threat of force. To the third question, Hart argued that the relation is necessary and constitutive: law is, at its foundation, everywhere and always grounded in social rules. By my count, identification and explanation of contingent relations constitute two-thirds of Hart's explanation of the concept of law.

Second, it may also help to alleviate some misgivings by noting that Hart's, and most of the interesting explanations of the concept of law, are philosophical constructions or what I have elsewhere called philosophically constructed concepts of law (Giudice, 2015, ch. 3). A philosophically constructed concept of law must of course remain true to the nature or reality of law; but as a philosophical construction with aspirations of universality, it can be constructed in any number of ways designed to illuminate its object and respond to various interests. A philosophically constructed concept of law can be fruitfully constructed out of a combination and balance of necessary and contingent features and relations, so long as these are meant to explain law wherever and whenever it exists.

Third, and perhaps most importantly, including contingent relations in a philosophical explanation of the concept of law is not some kind of philosophical trick or sleight of hand, but serves the purpose of maintaining and emphasizing the continuity of conceptual and empirical investigations. Far too often, theorists feel the need to swing the pendulum back and forth, emphasizing one at the expense of the other, or shoehorning one into the other. Conceptual and empirical questions about law are indeed different kinds of questions, but they are related, and their respective answers have the potential for mutual influence in a variety of ways.

To see, through the use of a philosophically constructed concept of law that includes contingent relations and features, that coercive means are possible but not necessary for the existence and operation of law, together with empirical knowledge about the conditions of success of coercion securing obedience, is also vital for showing the continuity of conceptual and empirical approaches with evaluative ones. For example, identification of some part of the existence and operation of law as contingent, and so capable of being otherwise, invites complementary moral evaluation to see when use of coercive means is morally justifiable or not (I am here assuming, among other things, that coercion is at least sometimes morally permissible or justifiable, that knowledge that it would be utterly ineffective under some conditions is morally relevant, etc.).

Obviously, much more needs to be said to explain and vindicate the kind of continuity I envisage here, as the most sensible, metatheoretical view of pluralism in legal theory. I have tried to do this in part in this Element and in a more sustained fashion elsewhere (Giudice, 2015; Giudice, 2020),[27] but in general I remain convinced that evaluative, conceptual, and empirical approaches are necessary approaches to understanding law, including its normativity, for each responds to a dimension of the very nature of law itself. Law is morally and prudentially significant in all the ways it can impact (for better or for worse) our interests, well-being, and lives, so evaluation (of both moral and prudential kinds) is a necessary approach for any complete understanding. Law is also presented and understood through the use of numerous intersubjective concepts (rights, obligations, authority, and the concept of law itself), which all shape our thought and action, so a conceptual or descriptive–explanatory perspective is required as well. And law, as we know it, applies to and governs and influences flesh-and-blood human beings (among other beings) in numerous causally relevant ways ripe for investigation by empirical study. There can certainly be a kind of sublevel diversity within each of these three approaches, but at the most general level this three-dimensional pluralism is directly responsive to the three dimensions of the nature of law.

The normativity of law is a prime site for the deployment of pluralism and continuity in legal theory. First, it matters, as a descriptive–explanatory or conceptual matter of social fact, how law presents itself as a kind of claim on our practical reason. Is it trying to do so in a distinctive way by settling for us what we ought to do as our best course of action? Is its claim of the same structure and character in all instances? Second, thinking not of how law presents itself, but how it lands or is received, are there particular reasons (e.g., prudence) or forms of persuasion (e.g., threats of force) that are more likely to result in compliance? If more than one kind of reason is typically required, what combination of reasons might work best to secure obedience, and how might such a combination need to vary across different contexts? Unlike

---

[27] See also Julie Dickson's notion of "staged inquiry" in Dickson, 2022, ch. 7.

the first set of questions, it is reasonable to suppose that this second set is not primarily philosophical, but psychological or sociological instead. What is not reasonable is to suppose that because such questions are not primarily philosophical they are not about the normativity of law. It is also not reasonable to suppose that answers to empirical questions might not give us reasons to adjust or revise our conceptual explanations; empirical investigations could draw attention to better ways of framing conceptual questions, or even show that what we might have taken to be a conceptual feature of law is better understood as an empirical generalization with important exceptions. Third, as the lists of Bix, Dickson, Green, and others acknowledge, understanding when and why the law morally obligates us is a central part of understanding the normativity of law. It is also a part that works in close partnership with conceptual explanations (what exactly are we asking about when we ask if *law* morally obligates?) and empirical studies (assuming, as I do, that empirical conditions are relevant to moral assessment of one's obligations and obedience to law). The normativity of law thus provides a superb illustration of the possibility and value of continuity in legal theory.

9 Future Directions

This final section sets out a range of possible investigations into the normativity of law. Some are best understood as amplifications of existing work, while others point to somewhat newer territory for legal theory. Using the framework identified in Section 8, I believe there are new directions to take within and across the three main types of approach and method: conceptual, evaluative, and empirical.

9.1 Conceptual

There is much work to be done in analyzing the kinds of claims that law makes on its subjects as practical reasoners. I suggested in Part I that theorists such as Aquinas, Finnis, and Raz were right to see that human law sometimes presents a certain choice or concretization of general moral values, but whether the role of human law is best understood simply as "determining" general moral values or as "excluding" appeal to first-order reasons remains to be assessed. Recently, David Enoch offered an intriguing account: that law, or legal reasons, are "triggering reasons" in the sense that once a particular law has been created, which can now serve as a legal reason, it is best explained as having triggered an underlying or latent moral reason (Enoch, 2011). For example, before a particular rule is established that tells us on which side of the road to drive, there is both a dormant or untriggered moral reason to drive on the left side of the road and a dormant or untriggered moral reason to drive on the right side of the road. But once a rule is laid down – for example, "drive on the right side of the road" – this rule serves to trigger (and so can be understood as a triggering reason) the latent or untriggered moral reason to drive on the right side of the road, which now becomes the active moral reason. In Enoch's view, before laws are posited, there can be an indefinite number of dormant, conditional, untriggered moral reasons, which do not yet have any force but will if triggered by particular laws. Enoch's view is not without its critics (Ehrenberg, 2016, 154–60), but it does signal that more work is needed to explain precisely how we ought to conceptualize this particular relation between law and morality – namely, how we are to understand and articulate the role that positive law plays in drawing or relying on moral standards.[28] It is also, I would submit, a more interesting and more important conceptual question than thinking about whether unjust laws are really laws.

There is another familiar topic I believe is ripe for conceptual reconsideration, and which centers around the question of political legitimacy. Typically, the question raised is one about the "right to rule," which invites morally evaluative approaches to try to show when such a right is legitimately wielded. But it is worth pausing, before launching into morally evaluative investigation, to ask whether the legitimacy of legal and political institutions is always or everywhere best framed as a question about the right to rule. For example, there might be value, in both descriptive explanation and subsequent moral assessment, in thinking about the legitimacy of legal and political institutions in terms of a duty or responsibility to govern (Green, 2007; Giudice and Schaeffer, 2012). It might of course be true that legal and political institutions claim a right to rule, but we need not always take such self-understandings at face value and as settling how subsequent moral assessment ought to be carried out. I might claim to be an accomplished soccer player, to family, friends, and strangers, but my professional success is better measured by my achievements (or their absence) as a philosopher.

There is a related area of conceptual investigation that is overdue for analysis. Must law always and everywhere be understood as claiming supreme and comprehensive authority? This question can be considered at a couple of levels. One is the international level. Much international law is of a hortatory kind and specifies several ideals, from human rights to climate harm mitigation, for example, which then act as standards for states to meet. But most states must implement international agreements and conventions for them to be operable and justiciable within state borders. Some might then claim that this shows

---

[28] See Rosen, 2013, for a challenge to the particular way in which Joseph Raz constructs his theory of law's authority and exclusionary reasons for action.

international law is not really law (another tired question, I am afraid); but an alternative possibility might be to question whether law must everywhere and always claim to be authoritative. International laws typically have social sources, which serve as objects of recognition and reference, so it could be that we must rethink the type of normative claim that international law makes and avoid using models of legal normativity developed exclusively from the context of the sovereign state.

Another level is intra- or substate, and here I have in mind contexts where state governments are coming to terms with colonial histories and the injustice these have leveled (and continue to level) against Indigenous peoples. One of the dimensions of work in such states is to recognize properly the rights of self-government and inherent jurisdiction of Indigenous peoples, and in a way that does not simply subsume Indigenous legal orders under the supreme and comprehensive authority of state legal systems. This requires much work to question the very concept of legal system, and the kinds of assertions associated with its presence in political communities (Giudice, 2020, ch. 4).

9.2 Evaluative

With regard to morally evaluative investigations, some follow directly from the questions and issues just raised. For example, in places where there are multiple legal orders and governments that claim foundational or constitutional author-ity, such as one finds in New Zealand and Canada, where relations between state and Indigenous governments are being reimagined, we likely need to reformu-late the conditions of political legitimacy. Nicole Roughan, in her important book *Authorities*, has begun such important work by offering an account of "relative authority" in which she argues that where certain forms of legal pluralism are present, one of the conditions of legitimate governance – that is, one of the conditions for satisfying the moral normativity of law – is cooper-ation or coordination among the various governments or institutions that must share authority.[29]

Another future direction of evaluative analysis of law's normativity ties it directly to advances in technology, and particularly artificial intelligence (AI). Information communication technologies offer vast amounts of information at our fingertips, like never before, and, together with recent applications of AI, it is not unreasonable to suppose that instant legal advice, or access to immediately available identification of laws, is close, perhaps in the familiar form of a smartphone application. Such an

---

[29] In Roughan's words, "To say that law claims relative authority rather than independent authority is to say that law claims authority that is conditional upon appropriate relationships between its legal institutions and others with which it shares authority" (Roughan, 2013, 154).

advance could reasonably be lauded as a rule-of-law improvement, saving citizens the time and expense of seeking legal advice in light of their ignorance of law and instead providing them with real-time knowledge of their legal rights and obligations. But is more knowledge of law necessarily and always a good thing? Perhaps not. It might be good for citizens not to know (or take an active interest in knowing) the specifics of their legal obligations on some occasions, and to act instead on the basis of general moral values (not to harm others, to keep promises, to maintain standards of care, etc.).[30] Knowing too much about law and its consequences, or the chances of getting caught for breaking the law, could encourage types of cost–benefit analysis that we are morally better off without. Think of the rule-of-law requirement that law on the books should match law in action, upset or compromised by a "police presence alert" smartphone application, which would support actions to avoid detection. Think also of someone looking to do harm to another but not to excess, calibrating the exact amount and kind of harm they will inflict on the basis of real-time knowledge at their fingertips of the precise degrees and kinds of civil and criminal assault. Again, it might be better from a moral point of view (and possibly a prudential point of view as well) not to know the specific conditions of legal wrongs and to act instead on more general moral notions of right and wrong as a matter of habit and disposition.[31]

9.3 Empirical

Technological advancements are just one example of how empirical conditions can alter the circumstances under which law operates and makes demands on subjects, and how subjects might in turn relate to the normative claims they face. Other types of conditions include environmental events, such as droughts, fires, floods, and earthquakes, which all ought to be studied to see how and when they upset legal order and alter the success of law's claims on subjects.[32] One further

---

[30] Leslie Green offers a similar observation:

> Remember that normative guidance is only one way that law contributes to society, and it is not always its best way. Consider sexual assault. Does law's contribution to sexual morality go best when it prescribes sound norms about consent, and everyone *takes those norms* as their reason for responding properly to their partner's interests? ("I must not get her too drunk to consent to sex – that would violate the law!") As Bernard Williams used to say, that is "one thought too many." Better that law should indirectly, and sometimes non-normatively, affect the ordinary social norms that guide sexual interaction. Likewise, we want people to avoid assault, to refrain from discrimination, and to deal fairly, not because of a lively awareness of the normative force of law, but because it would hardly occur to them to do otherwise. (Green, 2023, 21)

[31] The kind of danger I have in mind here is somewhat materialized when professional ethics are turned into detailed codes and subsequently treated as comprehensive rule books to be followed at the expense of developing a strong sense of moral principle.

[32] For descriptive–explanatory exploration of law's relations to security, technology, and the environment, see Culver and Giudice, 2017.

type of investigation that should be included in understanding the normativity of law would be the construction of better tools to scan for when, where, and why new forms of legal order, at all levels – from local to regional, state, and global – are likely to emerge or ought to be established. State breakdown or failure, or regions impacted by natural and human-made disasters, typically display a kind of "normative need" for law, since such events typically signal or indicate a collapse of existing legal orders, so needing new or outside institutions to provide support or create new legal order. Such study would thus require development of the idea of "normative need" and use it to detect when, where, and why legal order is likely to emerge or should be sought. (The cyber domain is another prime example where activity has been far outstripping legal regulation, and so exhibits strong normative need.)

As we saw in Section 7, I have placed psychological and predictive accounts, though focused squarely on coercion, as key accounts (among others) in any broad understanding of the normativity of law. But such social scientific accounts need to be widened even further, to include not just a broader spectrum of causal influences on humans as they relate to law, but also to explore more completely the ways in which legal norms relate to other types of norms. The Covid-19 pandemic brought into sharp relief just how important it is to have some legal norms (about vaccination, masking, physical distancing, etc.) translate, quickly and effectively, into new social norms. What did we learn about how to make new legal norms immediately effective as social norms to face the challenges of rapidly spreading viruses? At the very least, that it is no easy feat. Creating social change with law represents an important aspect of the normativity of law, and one whose explanation demands our best efforts.

These are just some examples of areas where theoretical attention to the normativity of law could be developed. Some might complain that the range of areas is too broad, so too unwieldly, for legal theory to address. This is true – I think the problems of the normativity of law are several, and the range of areas vast. But I propose a principle. The approaches that fall under each of the conceptual, evaluative, and empirical categories have for a very long time been carried out in isolation from approaches falling under the other categories. This has resulted in many missed opportunities for interaction, where accounts developed under one category could point towards revisions or reformulations of questions under another category. The principle is then to seek out, deliberately and in sustained fashion, intersections and points of continuity. Once again, I think Roughan's work is particularly instructive. In characterizing her account of relative authority, she writes:

> What is offered here might be considered a revisionist conception of authority . . .
> The problems with the existing concept not only reveal the need for revision of the
> concept itself but also, I think, the need for fresh conceptual analysis . . . This
> work, however, is not only engaged in conceptual analysis. It also offers a new
> theory of legitimate authority that is matched to the revised concept. There are
> thus two steps to the work, and it should be read as such. The first step argues
> that authority should be conceived as relative, shared, and interdependent, not
> binary, monist, or independent. The second argues that the legitimacy of such
> relative authority depends directly upon inter-relationships between authorities.
> (Roughan, 2013, 15)

Roughan's book exhibits precisely the kind of continuity between conceptual and morally evaluative approaches that I think will benefit from a pluralistic understanding of the normativity of law.

To return to two examples already mentioned, first, I think more work can be done to explore law's moral normativity through thinking about political legitimacy as a duty to govern instead of a right to rule. Though I cannot pursue it here, I suspect this might be more profitable, as it would highlight the need to think about the moral reasons to follow laws rather than obsessing about whether there is a general obligation to obey law, correlated with a government's right to rule. And second, if it is not true that law must always be conceived in the form of a state legal system, with its characteristic claims of comprehensiveness and supremacy over all other normative orders, then we might be better positioned to see other possibilities of how law could take shape in circumstances of legal pluralism, and in turn better achieve certain moral and political goals.

Conclusion

I am certainly not the first to suggest that the problem of the normativity of law is many, not one. Bix, Dickson, and Green, for example, have beaten me to that conclusion. But what is interesting about their lists of the various questions and problems of the normativity of law is that no two are exactly the same, and, more importantly, none include questions or problems to do with the empirical or social scientific dimensions of law's normativity. This omission alone, I believe, justifies an account that is broader in scope. I have also suggested that we need sustained attention to how the various kinds of approaches to the normativity of law relate to each other, how they combine, and how their pursuit can prompt mutual adjustment and sometimes abandonment of certain claims. Part of this task involves sorting out just what kind of claims are being assessed. At a general level, conceptual, evaluative, and empirical approaches are complementary and all required for a complete understanding of the normativity of law. There is no conflict at this level. But the possibility of conflict, or dispute, is possible at the level of particular propositions. For example, do judges necessarily believe they have a moral reason to follow the law when they decide cases before them? Raz thinks so, as it is a conceptual truth about the authoritative claims of law (though of course he acknowledges that judges could be substantively mistaken in their beliefs) (Raz, 2009b, 332). Hart disagreed and thought such a view was an empirical claim, and a false one at that (Hart, 2012, 203; Hart, 1982, 265). No consensus has emerged among later theorists, though perhaps if moral psychology advances far enough it might offer some insights.

I have also been very deliberate in putting breadth ahead of depth in this Element. Too often in the philosophy of law, extremely intricate and complex accounts are offered, which, in the interest of going as deep as they can, have fabricated problems about the normativity of law or failed to notice agreement across theories upon or after which new problems could be pursued. This has resulted in much stagnation in the philosophy of law, and no small amount of misdirected effort. I am convinced that observing a core area of agreement between natural law theory and legal positivism – that to establish whether there are moral reasons to comply with positive law requires an account of moral reasons that are external to law – is an important vaccination against the thought that explanations of law's moral or robust force can be found by drawing on resources within positive law itself, as folks as varied as Dworkin, Fuller, Coleman, and Shapiro suppose. If someone were to ask "What moral, or genuine reasons do I have for following the law, or accepting the consequences of its operation?" it would be more than a little odd to begin a response with "Well, the law displays an impeccable level of clarity ..." or "When our beliefs and intentions align, this can create reasons for action for each of us to ..." Such answers may end up quite deep but have perhaps dug in the wrong places or mistakenly presumed digging was necessary in the first place. A broader look at what we have learned in the philosophy of law, or what we have agreed on – which becomes visible when we are not overly excited by disagreement – is needed for some balance.

I have also insisted throughout this Element that we should guard against the disposition to narrow how the problem of the normativity of law is conceived. It is true that analytical legal theory needs to be rigorous and precise in making distinctions in search of the core of particular problems. But such distinctions and searching need not always mean that one problem, and only one problem, must be declared the winner, as the one and only problem that matters. In the case of the problem of the normativity of law, there are actually many problems, with various dimensions and relations. Law, including its normativity, is interesting in several ways and for many reasons. We need an account that respects this fact and offers a way to study and appreciate it properly.

References

Aquinas, St. T. (2017). "Treatise on Law" from *Summa Theologica*. In K. Culver and M. Giudice, eds., *Readings in the Philosophy of Law*, 3rd ed. Peterborough, ON: Broadview Press, pp. 27–40.

Aristotle (2009). *The Nicomachean Ethics*. Translated by W. D. Ross, edited by L. Brown. Oxford: Oxford University Press.

Austin, J. (2000). *The Province of Jurisprudence Determined*. Amherst, NY: Prometheus.

Bentham, J. (1987). Anarchical Fallacies. In J. Waldron, ed., *"Nonsense upon Stilts": Bentham, Burke, and Marx on the Rights of Man*. London: Methuen.

Bix, B. (2005). Legal Positivism. In M. P. Golding, ed., *The Blackwell Guide to the Philosophy of Law and Legal Theory*. Oxford: Blackwell Publishing, pp. 29–49.

Bratman, M. (1992). Shared Cooperative Activity. *Philosophical Review*, 101(2), 327–41.

Coleman, J. (2001). *The Practice of Principle*. Oxford: Oxford University Press.

Cotterrell, R. (2017). *Sociological Jurisprudence*. London: Routledge.

Culver, K., and Giudice, M. (2017). *The Unsteady State*. New York: Cambridge University Press.

Dickson, J. (2001). *Evaluation and Legal Theory*. Oxford: Hart Publishing.

Dickson, J. (2022). *Elucidating Law*. Oxford: Oxford University Press.

Dworkin, R. (1978). *Taking Rights Seriously*. Cambridge, MA: Harvard University Press.

Dworkin, R. (1986). *Law's Empire*. Cambridge, MA: Harvard University Press.

Dyzenhaus, D. (2022). *The Long Arc of Legality*. Cambridge: Cambridge University Press.

Ehrenberg, K. (2016). *The Functions of Law*. Oxford: Oxford University Press.

Emon, A. (2010). *Islamic Natural Law Theories*. Oxford: Oxford University Press.

Enoch, D. (2011). Reason-Giving and the Law. In L. Green and B. Leiter, eds., *Oxford Studies in Philosophy of Law: Volume 1*. Oxford: Oxford University Press, pp. 1–38.

Finnis, J. (1980). *Natural Law and Natural Rights*. Oxford: Clarendon Press.

Finnis, J. (1998). *Aquinas*. Oxford: Oxford University Press.

Fuller, L. (1969). *The Morality of Law*, rev. ed. New Haven, CT: Yale University Press.

Gardner, J. (2012). *Law as a Leap of Faith*. Oxford: Oxford University Press.

Gauthier, D. (1986). *Morals by Agreement*. Oxford: Clarendon Press.

Giudice, M. (2015). *Understanding the Nature of Law*. Cheltenham: Edward Elgar.

Giudice, M. (2016). Imperialism and Importance in Dworkin's Jurisprudence. In W. Waluchow and S. Sciaraffa, eds., *The Legacy of Ronald Dworkin*. Oxford: Oxford University Press, pp. 225–43.

Giudice, M. (2019). Review of Kenneth Ehrenberg, *The Functions of Law* (Oxford University Press, 2016). *Philosophical Quarterly*, 69(277), 864–67.

Giudice, M. (2020). *Social Construction of Law*. Cheltenham: Edward Elgar.

Giudice, M., and Schaeffer, M. (2012). Universal Jurisdiction and the Duty to Govern. In F. Tanguay-Renaud and J. Stribopoulos, eds., *Rethinking Criminal Law Theory*. Oxford: Hart Publishing, pp. 233–48.

Gkouvas, T. (2023). *The Place of Coercion in Law*. Cambridge: Cambridge University Press.

Green, L. (2007). The Duty to Govern. *Legal Theory*, 13(3–4), 165–85.

Green, L. (2008). Positivism and the Inseparability of Laws and Morals. *New York University Law Review*, 83(4), 1035–58.

Green, L. (2023). The Normativity of Law: What is the Problem? www.uvic.ca/victoria-colloquium/assets/docs/Green_Normativity.pdf.

Greenberg, M (2014). The Moral Impact Theory of Law. *Yale Law Journal*, 123(5), 1288–343.

Hart, H. L. A. (1958). Legal and Moral Obligation. In A. I. Melden, ed., *Essays in Moral Philosophy*. Seattle: Washington University Press, pp. 82–107.

Hart, H. L. A. (1982). *Essays on Bentham*. Oxford: Clarendon Press.

Hart, H. L. A. (1983). *Essays in Jurisprudence and Philosophy*. Oxford: Clarendon Press.

Hart, H. L. A. (2012). *The Concept of Law*, 3rd ed. Oxford: Oxford University Press.

Himma, K. (2020). *Coercion and the Nature of Law*. Oxford: Oxford University Press.

Hobbes, T. (1985). *Leviathan*. Edited by C. B. Macpherson. London: Penguin Books.

Kelsen, H. (1970). *Pure Theory of Law*, 2nd ed. Translated by M. Knight. Berkeley, CA: University of California Press.

Kramer, M. (2004). *Where Law and Morality Meet*. Oxford: Oxford University Press.

Mackie, J. L. (1977). The Third Theory of Law. *Philosophy and Public Affairs*, 7(1), 3–16.

Postema, G. (1987). The Normativity of Law. In R. Gavison, ed., *Issues in Contemporary Legal Philosophy*. Oxford: Clarendon Press, pp. 81–104.

Rawls, J. (1971). *A Theory of Justice*. Cambridge, MA: Harvard University Press.

Raz, J. (1995). *Ethics in the Public Domain*, rev. ed. Oxford: Clarendon Press.

Raz, J. (1999). *Practical Reason and Norms*, 2nd ed. Oxford: Clarendon Press.

Raz, J. (2009a). *The Authority of Law*, 2nd ed. Oxford: Oxford University Press.

Raz, J. (2009b). *Between Authority and Interpretation*. Oxford: Oxford University Press.

Rosen, A. (2013). The Normative Fallacy Regarding Law's Authority. In S. Sciaraffa and W. Waluchow, eds., *Philosophical Foundations of the Nature of Law*. Oxford: Oxford University Press, pp. 75–100.

Roughan, N. (2013). *Authorities*. Oxford: Oxford University Press.

Russell, B. (1990). *The Problems of Philosophy*. Indianapolis, IN: Hackett Publishing.

Schauer, F. (2015). *The Force of Law*. Cambridge, MA: Harvard University Press.

Shapiro, S. (2011). *Legality*. Cambridge, MA: Harvard University Press.

Simmons, A. J. (1979). *Moral Principles and Political Obligations*. Princeton, NJ: Princeton University Press.

Smith, M. B. E. (1973). Is There a Prima Facie Obligation to Obey the Law? *Yale Law Journal*, 82(5), 950–76.

Tamanaha, B. (2001). *A General Jurisprudence of Law and Society*. Oxford: Oxford University Press.

Twining, W. (2009). *General Jurisprudence*. Cambridge: Cambridge University Press.

Waluchow, W. (1994). *Inclusive Legal Positivism*. Oxford: Clarendon Press.

Williams, K. P. (2018). *Kayanerenkó:wa*. Winnipeg, MB: University of Manitoba Press.

Woodbury-Smith, K. (2020). The Nature of Law and Potential Coercion. *Ratio Juris*, 33(2), 223–40.

Yankah, E. (2008). The Force of Law: The Role of Coercion in Legal Norms. *University of Richmond Law Review*, 42(5), 1195–256.

Cambridge Elements ☰

Philosophy of Law

Series Editors

George Pavlakos
University of Glasgow

George Pavlakos is Professor of Law and Philosophy at the School of Law, University of Glasgow. He has held visiting posts at the universities of Kiel and Luzern, the European University Institute, the UCLA Law School, the Cornell Law School and the Beihang Law School in Beijing. He is the author of *Our Knowledge of the Law* (2007) and more recently has co-edited *Agency, Negligence and Responsibility* (2021) and *Reasons and Intentions in Law and Practical Agency* (2015).

Gerald J. Postema
University of North Carolina at Chapel Hill

Gerald J. Postema is Professor Emeritus of Philosophy at the University of North Carolina at Chapel Hill. Among his publications count *Utility, Publicity, and Law: Bentham's Moral and Legal Philosophy* (2019); *On the Law of Nature, Reason, and the Common Law: Selected Jurisprudential Writings of Sir Matthew Hale* (2017); *Legal Philosophy in the Twentieth Century: The Common Law World* (2011), *Bentham and the Common Law Tradition*, 2nd edition (2019).

Kenneth M. Ehrenberg
University of Surrey

Kenneth M. Ehrenberg is Professor of Jurisprudence and Philosophy at the University of Surrey School of Law and Co-Director of the Surrey Centre for Law and Philosophy. He is the author of *The Functions of Law* (2016) and numerous articles on the nature of law, jurisprudential methodology, the relation of law to morality, practical authority, and the epistemology of evidence law.

Associate Editor

Sally Zhu
University of Sheffield

Sally Zhu is a Lecturer in Property Law at University of Sheffield. Her research is on property and private law aspects of platform and digital economies.

About the Series

This series provides an accessible overview of the philosophy of law, drawing on its varied intellectual traditions in order to showcase the interdisciplinary dimensions of jurisprudential enquiry, review the state of the art in the field, and suggest fresh research agendas for the future. Focussing on issues rather than traditions or authors, each contribution seeks to deepen our understanding of the foundations of the law, ultimately with a view to offering practical insights into some of the major challenges of our age.

Cambridge Elements ≡

Philosophy of Law